Native American Magick

The Demons of Success

SINGLE VOLUME

Lucifer Faustus

ISBN: **9798867217174**

Lucifer Faustus 2023

All rights reserved

NATIVE AMERICAN MAGICK

The Demons of Success

SINGLE VOLUME

Copyright © 2023 Lucifer Faustus

All rights reserved

DISCLAIMER:

The information in this book is provided for informational purposes only. The author and those involved in the production of the work are not responsible for anyone who uses the information in this book for illegal activities or if any person is injured or harmed by the use of the information contained herein.

CONTENTS

Gallery 11
Introduction 19
The Mapanaith Demons 23
Learning to Get the Right Result 27
Before the Ritual 29
Firming the Energy in Place 33
Tracing the Portal 37
Sacred Writings 39
Closing the Ritual 43
Knowing the Demonic Gods Mapanaith 45
Zugbhath 47
Pantath 57
Namashiph 65
Tanbherini 73
Dhithupo 81
Garina 89
Dirindho 97
Makhisth 105
Hifh 113
Paranga 121
Shonzalorth 129
Poratha 137

Onpahan	147
Halh	155
Vanoilth	163
Meltrafon	171
Noabhind	179
Bhoran	187
Nathandha	195
Hanthal	203
Shisthenoalgho	211
Malentha	219
Khoril	227
Patheo	235
Chrisnonbh	243
Thimuel	253
Kuombho	263
Odhinga	271
Nebhituagh	281
Nirondhi	291
Bhaldondhi	301
Yanklauthemar	311
Maranghonebhiros	319
Thedhiongharitha	329
Ritual of Success and Victory with Shamanic Magick	337

Ritual to Defeat the Enemy with Shamanic Magick 345

Gallery

In this chapter I will share some pictures that I took during the development of the Shamanic Magick Mapanaith adaptation.

It is possible to notice in the photos that some portals are different from what was shown in the previous chapters. Several Mapanaith Demons can be contacted with several different types of portals, plus each portal and each Demon that was described in the book they were described in this way because they are the most efficient way to practice this magick.

Now I share with you the pictures taken during the adaptation tests of the Magick System.

Namashiph

Tanbherini

Paranga

Pantath

Kuombho

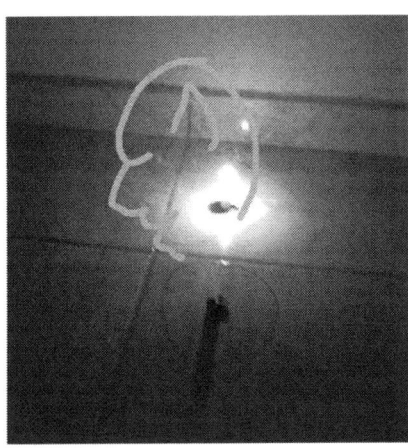

Halh

Garina

Introduction

When I decided to write this book, I was very excited, but I knew it was a big responsibility and that it would be a little complex to gather all the important information in one place.

Putting it all together, the existing written information, and the oral information that was most of everything I had related to these beings and their rituals. And the practical information of the magickal works that I have already done, and information of works that older wizards do.

In my youth I often used popular grimoires and the techniques taught in them, I found it much more exciting to do magickal work that I found in Solomon's Clavicles or in the Great Grimoire, than to use the Magickal wisdom of my ancestors.

At one point in my magickal journey, those magickal systems no longer seemed as exciting as they did in my teens, and I began to see that I had stumbled across my life in something magnificent. I was in front of me all the time and I couldn't see the range of knowledge and exciting possibilities that my people's magick system offered. I removed the blindfold from my eyes and immersed myself in the magickal knowledge of my ancestors.

Magick knowledge and years of practice with conventional systems were not wasted time for me, and as I delved deeper into shamanic magick, I was identifying similarities between that magic and the magick of my adolescence.

I came to the conclusion that Ars Goetia was an adaptation of something much older. In jewish magick the beings that are evoked are the 72 Daimons, in African magick the orixás are evoked, and there is an exact correspondence of the beings of the two magickal systems. In the magick of my people, I managed to identify the same correspondences, not for everyone. And that is what this book is about. I will list the telluric beings of my tribe with the evocation rituals and their correspondence with the 72 Daimons.

If you are a practitioner of Magick, you may notice in my rituals, similarities to conventional magickal grimoire systems, and this was done on purpose to facilitate the practice of everything that is taught in this book. The adaptations were made after tiring tests and did not affect the potency of the spell.

I will give you access to the oral Magick tradition of my ancestors, but make no mistake about the simplicity of the rituals, perhaps this is the most powerful thing you have ever had contact with. It's the most powerful thing I've ever manipulated, and it literally looks like a handful of explosives about to detonate.

The Mapanaith Demons

Mapanaith demons are telluric beings worshiped as gods in some tribes. And like demons in others.

I have worked with Mapanaith for several years, and my family has worked with them for generations.

Based on my experience with these telluric beings, my opinion is that they are Demonic Gods. If they like you, then you will see their divine aspect, more if they do not like you, then you will know their demonic aspect.

The Mapanaith are immensely powerful, and the purpose of their relationship with them is respect and worship on our part, in exchange for Wealth, power, love, health and destruction of enemies. The divine aspect of the Mapanaith in our favor and their demonic aspect against our enemies.

The Mapanaith were known among the people who worshiped them as war and plague lords, because they took people who did not worship pests and diseases and also defeat in wars.

I work with 34 Mapanaith and for generations Mapanaith shamanic magick practitioners have worked with this number of Demonic Gods. Perhaps other people who have inherited this magical system can worship a greater number of Mapanaith, or a smaller number, as most of the knowledge is passed on orally, it is possible that something has been lost over the generations.

In this book I will talk about the 34 Mapanaith Demons, I will address all these incredible beings.

All of the rituals in this book have been cleaned up and adapted to be accessible to anyone anywhere on the planet. So believe me when I say that this is powerful and is within your reach.

All Rituals were extensively tested in their adapted form, and 34 Mapanaith and its rituals were included in this book to ensure a high level of effectiveness and keep the practicing reader away from excessively dangerous rituals. But maybe in the future I decide to create a second volume of this book or a new edition with all the known Mapanaith and their respective rituals.

The 34 Demons in this book have many powers, so I have listed only the powers that I know work, as confirmed in my tests.

Sometimes, you will have the intuition that a Demon has a power that is not listed. You can try to make a wish to the demon and see what happens.

Working with these forces is not dangerous, as long as you follow the instructions. I am not discouraging you from making your own discoveries, but until you understand how the dynamics of Shamanic Magick work and how to work with the Mapanaith you must be cautious about tampering with the structure of the rituals.

Remember that Mapanaith are demons, be careful.

On each page, you will obtain the name of the demon in our tradition, the corresponding name in goetia, his powers and how to proceed in the evocation ritual.

The powers are described in short sentences, and the rituals are as clean as possible.

For each demon, there is a type of incense or mixture of incense, which are inside a geometric shape. Geometric shapes are not important, except to help you focus on what's inside and condense energy. Focus on the material placed inside the geometric shape.

Learning to Get the Right Result

The first step is to find the right demon to make your wish come true.

When you know what you want, you flip through the book and look for a Mapanaith that you think can help you. You just need to make sure that the demon's area of expertise is the right one, but you'll know what you need when you need it.

Sometimes a power calls for you, and that is a good sign. Sometimes you'll find a smarter way to get what you want, and that's a good thing too. The important thing is the correct result.

But how will you know what you want and what to order? and how to order?

The most common mistake is wanting to conquer everything at once. Go in stages, but use your common sense.

It is better to aim at a single duck and knock it down than to try to shoot everyone and not knock any.

Mapanaith Demons have immense power, but if you try to change the universe with a giant desire, nothing will happen and you may still seem disrespectful. Mapanaith are Demons, not angels. Watch out!

If you try to do 30 different rituals in a week focused on several different things, not much will happen either.

Look at your life, what makes you uncomfortable? Now imagine how this could change, and that is the desired result.

That's how you make magick work. And this is how you get the result you want.

If you are struggling to pay the bills, relieving your discomfort would come from paying the bills and getting out of debt. You don't have to win the lottery to make it happen, so don't waste your time on fantasies. The reality is much more satisfying.

This is a great example of how you find what you need, and you can solve anything like that. Look at your own needs, look at the powers and how they work and form the idea of the desired outcome that you want.

You can focus on really big changes with Magick, but if you're not prepared for them, it usually won't happen. Or if it does, you won't be able to maintain it.

Before the Ritual

When you believe in the true power of Magick, it works. If you see this detail as nonsense, and do the work of Magick mechanically, it probably won't work.

You must be aware that what you are going to do is something serious and will always have results, whether positive or negative.

When I say that the Magick will not work I mean when the magic brings a bad result. You may not even realize it, but the Magick of this book always generates a result, and the result of a poorly performed ritual will always fall on someone, if it is not you, it will fall on someone who has some connection with you, your neighbor or your cousin, Your Friend. And that is why, on some occasions, Shamanic Magick seems to have had no effect.

Imagine yourself doing a destruction ritual for your enemy, and you accidentally forget a detail during the ritual. This could result in a reverse effect on your enemy, and instead of destroying him, you would strengthen him. This is something perfectly possible to happen, so I warn you again, be aware of what you are doing during the ritual and do not be distracted. It is your dreams that are at stake and your future.

Nobody likes to prepare for a Magickal Ritual. There is so much easy magic where you can perform a ritual in five minutes. So why should you be concerned? Just take one of these easy rituals on the internet and perform it and be happy. Is not it?

You could just do that and sit around waiting for the result. With spells that don't work the internet is full, but if you want something that really works, here it is!

You may also be tempted to skip any part of this book, especially the preparation part, and move on to the rituals part. If you do, you will surely wonder why the Magick produced a different result than what you asked for, or worse, why it produced a totally negative result. And you will blame the Magick when it was you who failed to have the focus needed to prepare. It is your dreams that are at stake, would taking less time to focus on this cause be less important than being frustrated for the rest of your life? I think not.

So, here's the truth: I came to the conclusion that some preparation helps with the results of the Magick.

It's easier than you think. You do not need to spend a month praying or a week meditating. The only thing you need to do is spend some time achieving a certain degree of purification.

The purification necessary to contact a Mapanaith consists of clearing the mind of thoughts contrary to its purpose, and remaining free from distractions, bringing all your attention to the ritual. This makes you more visible to the demons, so that they will be open to your demands.

Get organized and enter a state that shows some respect for demons.

If you follow this advice you will be very close to a desired result.

Firming the Energy in Place

- To the north.
- Trace the double pentagram in the air and at the same time vibrate the words of power:

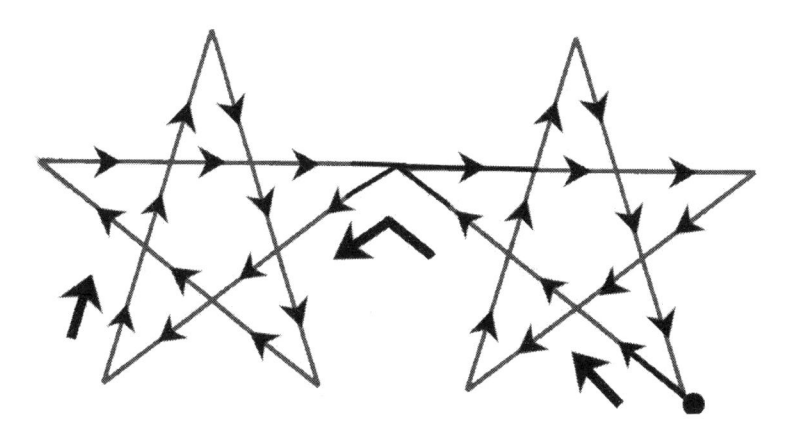

NAHAWAH KABIH OHAN DIATH SHIIBHA NOIIBHA BHAHAN

After preparing for the ritual by getting rid of distractions and concentrating, you will have to steady the energy of the elements by tracing the double pentagram in the air towards the north.

The double pentagram symbolizes the positive and negative aspects of the 5 elements, which are necessary to manipulate to harmonize the environment and make it favorable and pleasant for the demons.

I adapted the Golden Dawn technique of drawing pentagrams in the air, which was later used in Thelema, as it is more familiar to practitioners of magic at all levels.

In the original version of shamanic magic, the energies of the 5 elements and their positive and negative aspects are also manipulated, more in a much more complex and complicated way. When manipulating air, for example, you would blow with your own mouth, symbolizing the positive aspect of the air that brings your life. Then you would swallow the smoke from a pipe and blow in the same way as you did previously, symbolizing the negative aspect of the air that it can kill. The creative fire is the one that bakes food and the destructive fire is the one that incinerates life. And so on with the other elements.

I still open my rituals in the traditional way, but I also use the double pentagram in some situations where time is scarce and I need to save time and still perform powerful and powerful rituals quickly.

Perhaps in the future I will write a book describing the entire traditional procedure in detail, but this will depend on the acceptance of that book by the readers.

Tracing the Portal

> Facing north.

Start tracing the portal on the floor, clockwise. You will be facing north tracing the portal clockwise, but before finishing, leave the drawing open in the part closest to you. The south side of the portal. You will place the necessary materials for the ritual through the opening and then close the portal and finish the drawing.

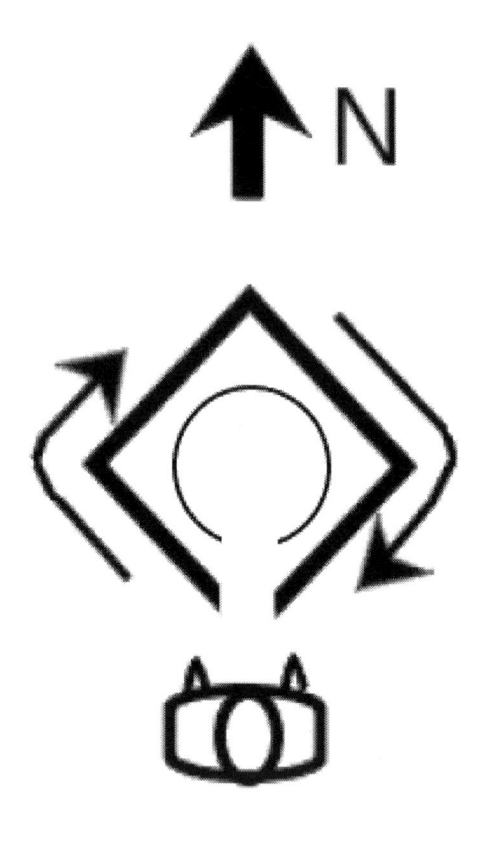

You will find detailed materials for each demon ahead.

For each Demon there is a specific geometric shape, which is the appropriate portal to contact Mapanaith efficiently.

Sacred Writings

After you have established the energy and balanced the environment by tracing the double pentagram, and tracing the portal on the floor leaving the south side open, you will now place the materials inside the portal.

After the portal is ready, you will trace the sacred writings on the portal.

The sacred writings are symbols and characters of the alphabet of the demonic language that serve as a key to open the portals and allow contact with the demon Mapanaith that you have chosen.

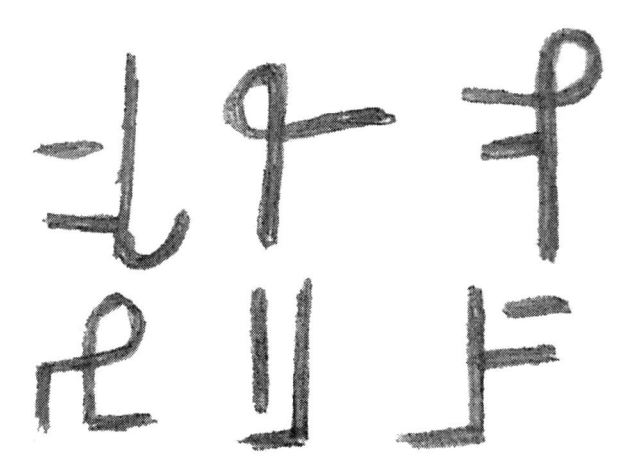

Each Mapanaith has its own set of sacred writings, and in the chapter where I present the twelve Mapanaith demons I will address each specific set of writing to unlock each portal.

The origin of sacred writing is uncertain and difficult to trace, considering that it has been passed down from generation to generation for centuries or perhaps millennia.

I doubt that these sacred characters were the result of human creation, due to their complexity and efficiency. Manipulating this writing in a ritual is like dialing a number on a cell phone and making a call. If the phone number contains an error, you will not be able to make the call.

To create this entire network and be able to communicate with another person anywhere on the planet, it took decades of investment and hard work in the areas of infrastructure and technology.

And how would you explain the fact that a tradition of at least a thousand years uses the principle of the telephone and remote communication in its rituals? In the case of magick we communicate with dimensional beings using the technology of characters and geometric shapes, which by the way is much more advanced than the technology of the cell phone communication network.

My guess is that the whole system of shamanic Magick that I use, was psychographed by some ancient shaman, who received this knowledge from very high beings, and that knowledge has been transmitted and preserved until today. And now I pass it on to you.

Closing the Ritual

- To the north.
- Trace the double pentagram in the air and at the same time vibrate the words of power:

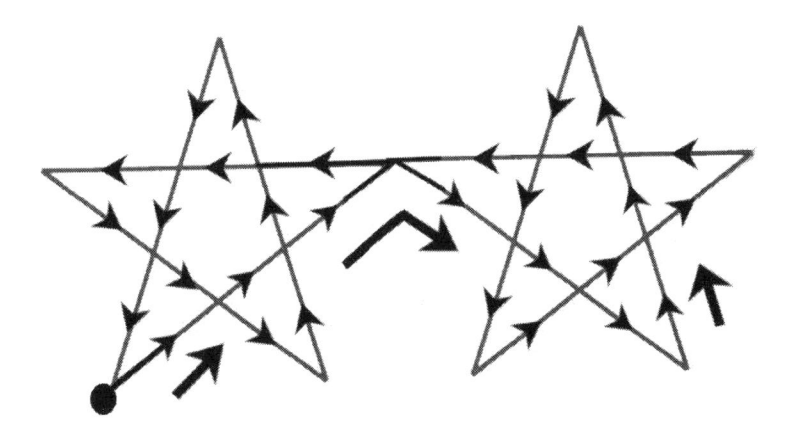

NAHAWAI NOHONAI NAMAHA NAMENIHI KOAN BHALIHI

After you complete the ritual, to finish everything and return to your normal routine you will have to draw the double closing pentagram to banish the forces and return to normality.

In the next chapter you will meet the 12 Mapanaith demons and I will cover the ritual in detail.

You will have a description of each demon and each step required to perform the ritual as in a cookbook. All you have to do is choose the demon who can help you, formulate a request and follow the steps exactly as shown.

This book could only contain the next chapter, and it would save me a great deal of time. But I thought it would be important to prepare you and prepare your mind before we get to the practical chapters.

Before performing any ritual in this book, you will at least have to be familiar with the double pentagram and know how to differentiate the opening pentagram from the closing pentagram. You will have to decorate that the portal is always designed in a clockwise direction and you will perform the entire ritual, from beginning to end, facing north.

Knowing the Demonic Gods Mapanaith

From that point on we will begin to know the 34 Mapanaith Demons, and will begin to learn about their specialties, powers and how to evoke them.

You have already become familiar with some terms used to refer to the Mapanaith and have already learned that they were known as "Warlords and the Plague", and to be called that way they had to be very powerful and feared. And they are! In fact, the correct term would be: powerful and dangerous. Terribly powerful and powerfully dangerous.

In our legends, they are responsible for making people like mine who worshiped them as Gods flourish, and for destroying the people who will oppose my people and the enemies of people who shared our belief.

Now that you know enough about this Magick system, let's move on to the practical Magick part.

Zugbhath

SPECIALTIES

- Cause fierce hatred between two named people.

- Bringing dissent to a group of people.
- Make a nominee lust after you
- Bring prosperity.
- Get wealth flow.
- Accumulate equity quickly.

GOETIA

- Corresponds to Gaap.

RITUAL

- To the north.
- Trace the double pentagram in the air and at the same time vibrate the words of power:

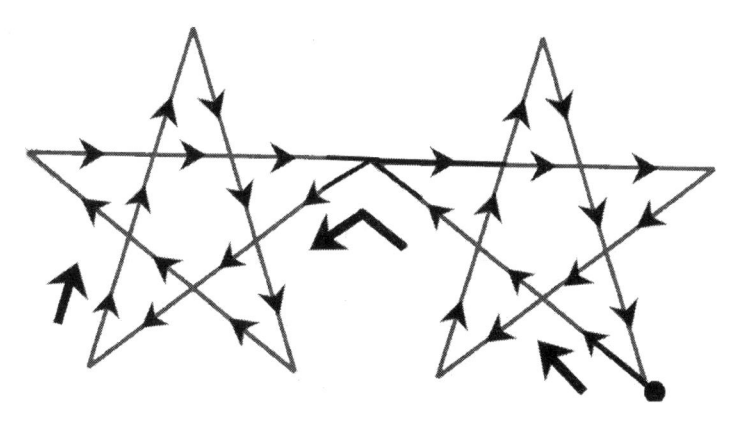

NAHAWAH KABIH OHAN DIATH SHIIBHA NOIIBHA BHAHAN

➢ Draw the portal clockwise and leave the south side of the portal open.

49

- Place **JASMINE** incense in the center of the circle and a **BLACK** candle inside the portal at the north end. Then light them.
- Finish the drawing by closing the portal.

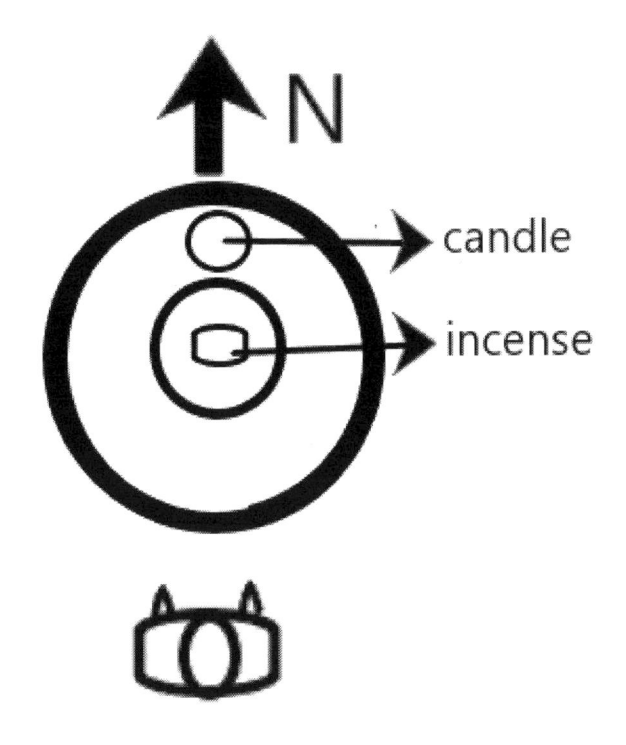

- Turn off the light.

- Pierce your finger and place 1 drop of blood inside the inner circle
- wait a few seconds

➤ Standing with your hands close to your body, recite the invitation:

KANIBHA THANIBHA HUABHI HASHIBHI HASHIBHU BANIBHU

➤ Wait a few seconds in silence.

➤ Draw the key in the air in front of the portal.

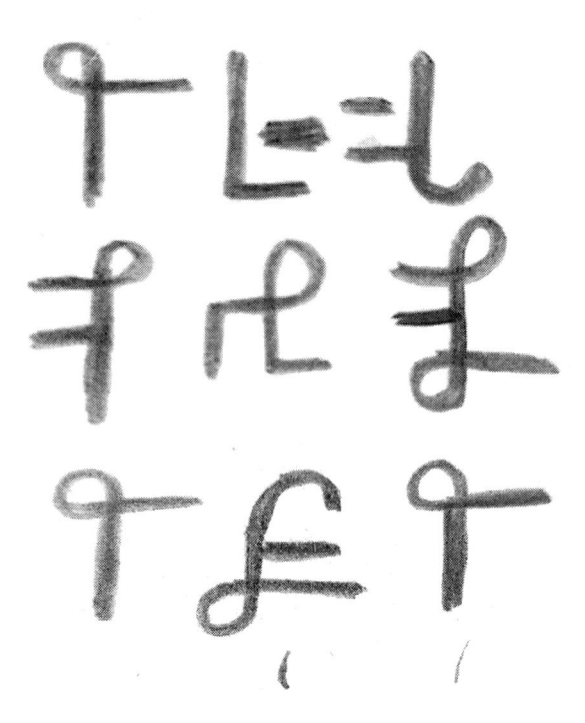

➤ Wait a few seconds.

- ➢ Now recite the evocation 3 times:

"ZUGBHATH KIV KARANA RIUNA SHOBHANA PAMDARAH"

- ➢ Wait a few minutes and if you don't feel the presence of Zugbhath repeat the above evocation 3 more times.
- ➢ Wait a few minutes.

- ➢ If Zugbhath has not yet manifested, recite the second evocation 3 times.

"KIV ZUGBHATH RIUNA KOAN NAGARA SHIBOM NANABHI"

- ➢ At the end of the third recitation it will be there, whether you feel it or not.
- ➢ Throw the piece of paper with your order inside the portal. You can write the request on paper before or at this time of the ritual, in the presence of Zugbhath.

- ➢ Envision the request for at least 5 minutes, imagine your request taking place, feel the emotion.
- ➢ After having mentalized, say:

"I thank Zugbhath for having heeded my call and I thank him for the request made."

- ➢ End the ritual.
- ➢ Trace the double pentagram in the air and at the same time vibrate the words of power:

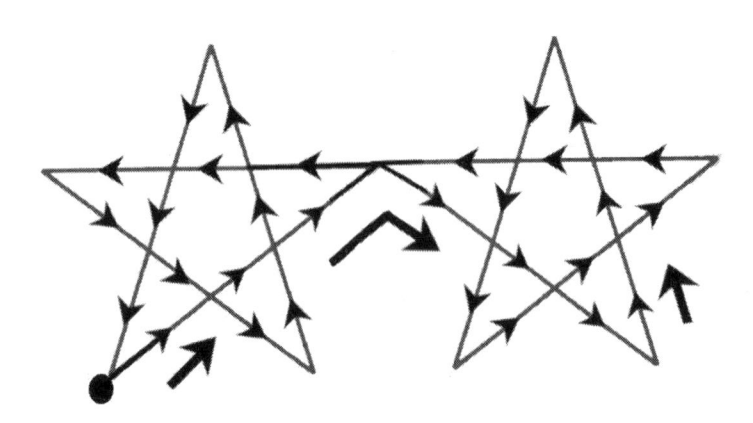

NAHAWAI NOHONAI NAMAHA NAMENIHI KOAN BHALIHI

- ➢ Leave the room and let the candle and incense burn to the end.

- Come back 24 hours later to clean everything up.
- Get back to your normal routine and wait for the results of the ritual without anxiety or doubt.

Pantath

SPECIALTIES

- Artistic Creativity.
- Fame and good reputation.
- Cause confusion.
- Make you feared and respected.
- Bring fame through art.
- Cause disgrace to a group of enemies.
- Lead several enemies to suicide at the same time.

GOETIA

- Corresponds to Forneus.

RITUAL

- To the north.
- Trace the double pentagram in the air and at the same time vibrate the words of power:

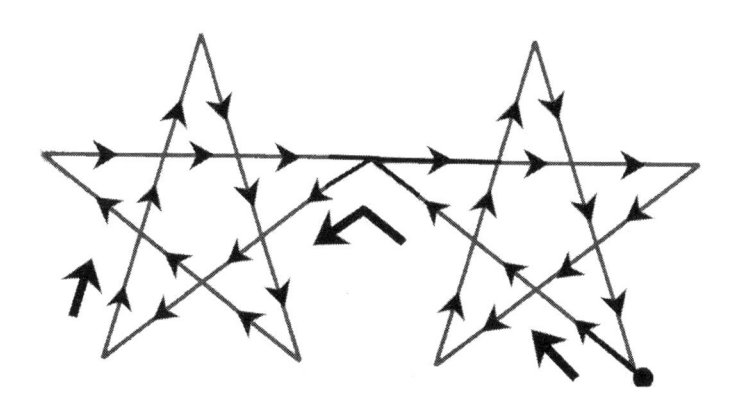

**NAHAWAH KABIH OHAN DIATH SHIIBHA
NOIIBHA BHAHAN**

- Draw the portal clockwise and leave the south side of the portal open.

- Place **MIRRA** incense in the center of the circle and a **WHITE** or **YELLOW** candle inside the outer design at the north end. Then light them up.
- Finish the drawing by closing the portal.

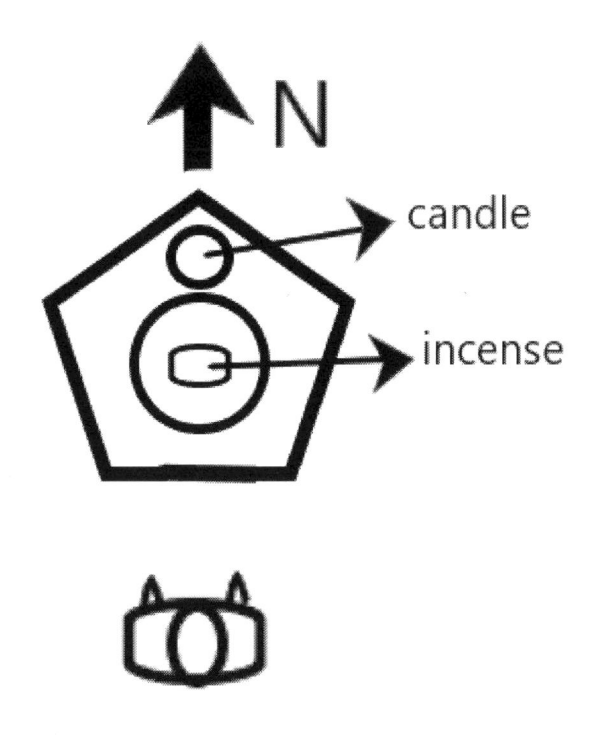

- Turn off the light.

- Standing with your hands at your sides, recite the invitation:

"THANIBHA HUANI SHIAN SHANABHI BHIASH"

- ➢ Wait a few seconds in silence.
- ➢ Draw the key in the air in front of the portal.

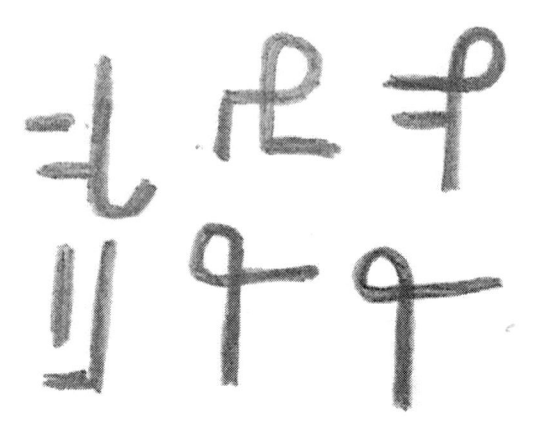

- ➢ Wait a few seconds.
- ➢ Now recite the evocation 3 times:

"KIU PANTATA PARAN RIUNA PANTATH RIUNA KOAN"

- ➢ Wait a few minutes and if you do not feel the presence of Pantath repeat the above evocation 3 more times.
- ➢ Wait a few minutes.

- If Pantath has not yet manifested himself, recite the second evocation 3 times.

"MANAH RIUNA KOAN TIBHARA PANTATH ARA PIN"

- At the end of the third recitation it will be there, whether you feel it or not.
- Throw the piece of paper with your order into the portal. You can write the order on paper before or at that time of the ritual, in the presence of Pantath.
- Mentalize the order for a minimum of 5 minutes, imagine your order being fulfilled, feel the emotion.
- After you have mentalized, say:

"I am grateful to Pantath for having heard my call and I am grateful for the request"

- End the ritual.
- Trace the double pentagram in the air and at the same time vibrate the words of power:

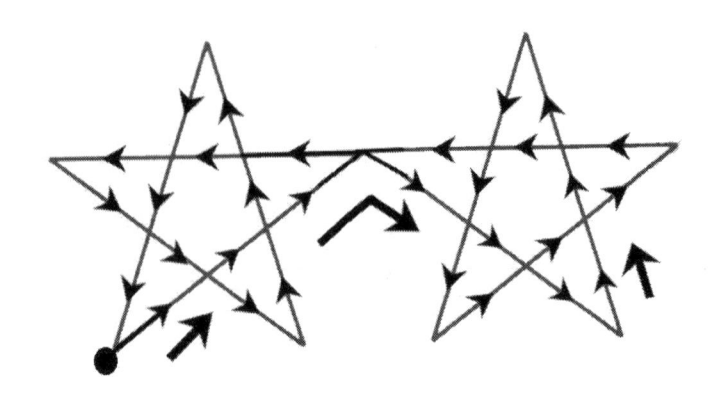

NAHAWAI NOHONAI NAMAHA NAMENIHI KOAN BHALIHI

- Exit the room and let the candle and incense burn to the end.
- Come back 24 hours later to clean up.
- Go back to your normal routine and wait for the results of the ritual without anxiety or doubt.

Namashiph

SPECIALTIES

- Obtain financial profit.
- Bring prosperity.
- Obtain wealth flow.
- Obtain material goods.
- Accumulate equity quickly.
- Lead enemies to misery.
- Make the enemy have financial losses.

GOETIA

- Corresponds to Bune.

RITUAL

- To the north.
- Trace the double pentagram in the air and at the same time vibrate the words of power:

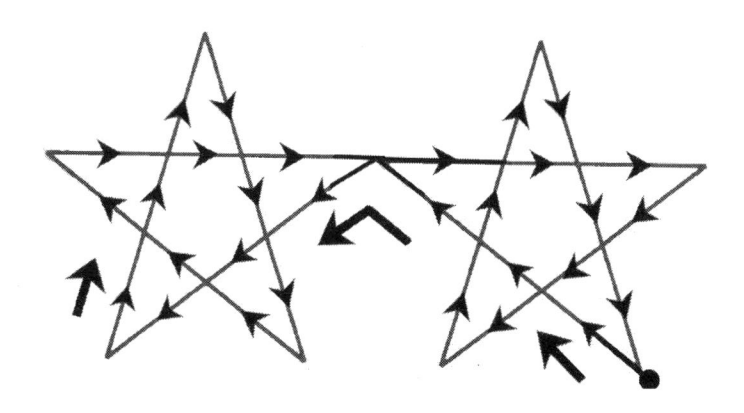

NAHAWAH KABIH OHAN DIATH SHIIBHA NOIIBHA BHAHAN

> Draw the portal clockwise and leave the south side of the portal open.

- Place the **ROSES** or **JASMINE** incense in the center of the circle and a **WHITE** or **ORANGE** candle inside the square at the north end. Then light them up.
- Finish the drawing by closing the portal.

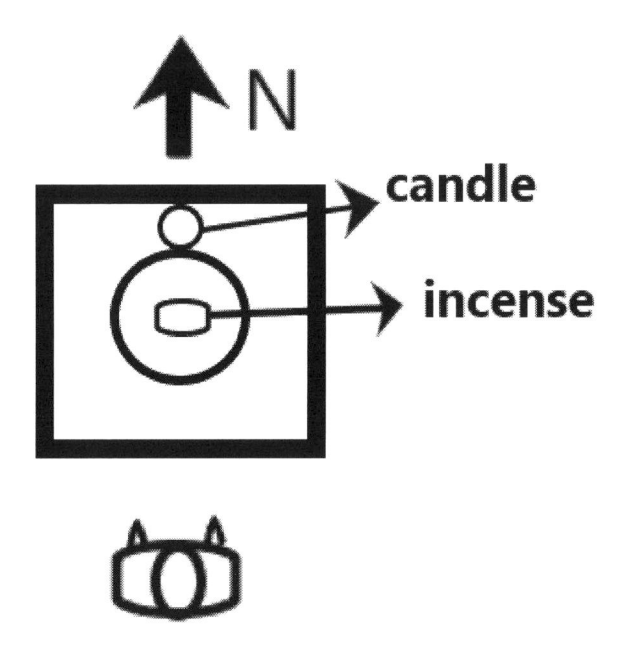

- Turn off the light.
- Standing with your hands at your sides, recite the invitation:

"KANIBHA THANIBHA HUABHI NANABHI HASHIBHU BANIBHU"

- Wait a few seconds in silence.
- Draw the key in the air in front of the portal

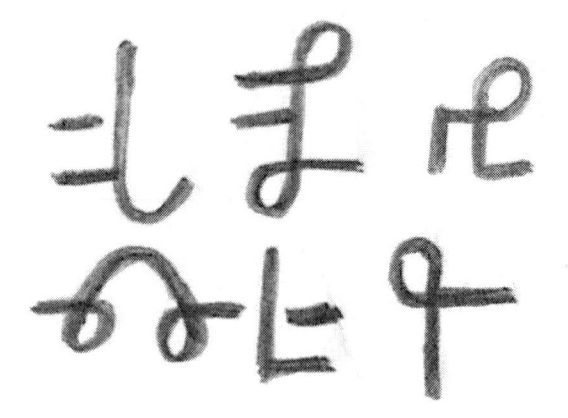

- ➢ Wait a few seconds.
- ➢ Now recite the evocation 3 times:

"KIV NAMASHIPH KARANA RIUNA KASHID SHORANA PAMDARAH"

- ➢ Wait a few minutes and if you do not feel the presence of Namashiph repeat the above evocation 3 more times.
- ➢ Wait a few minutes.

- If Namashiph has not yet manifested, recite the second evocation 3 times:

"NAMASHIPH RIUNA KOAN NAGARA SHIBOM"

- At the end of the third recitation it will be there, whether you feel it or not.
- Throw the piece of paper with your order into the portal. You can write the request on paper before or at that time of the ritual, in the presence of Namashiph.
- Mentalize the order for a minimum of 5 minutes, imagine your order being fulfilled, feel the emotion.
- After you have mentalized, say:

"I am grateful to Namashiph for having heard my call and I am grateful for the request made"

- End the ritual.
- Trace the double pentagram in the air and at the same time vibrate the words of power:

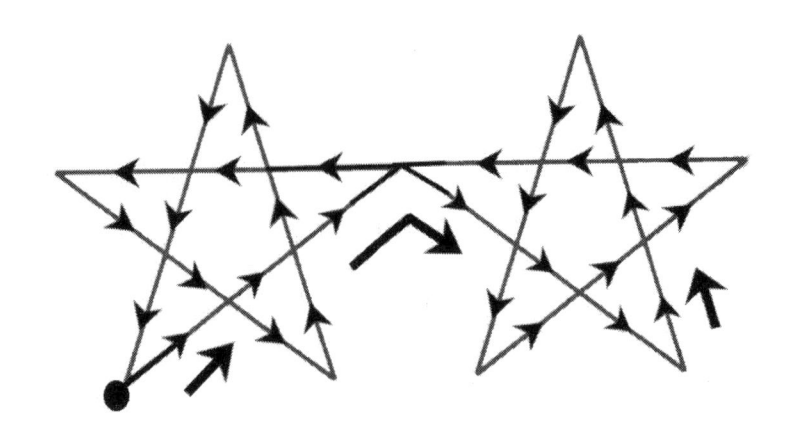

NAHAWAI NOHONAI NAMAHA NAMENIHI KOAN BHALIHI

- Exit the room and let the candle and incense burn to the end.
- Come back 24 hours later to clean up.
- Go back to your normal routine and wait for the results of the ritual without anxiety or doubt.

Tanbherini

SPECIALTIES

- Victory over enemies.

- Cause illusion of good reputation.
- Destruction of enemies.
- Demoralize and humiliate the enemy.
- Predict the future.
- Cause enemy suicide.
- Cause the enemy a slow and painful death.
- Lead the enemy to misery.

GOETIA

- Corresponds to Alloces.

RITUAL

- To the north.
- Trace the double pentagram in the air and at the same time vibrate the words of power:

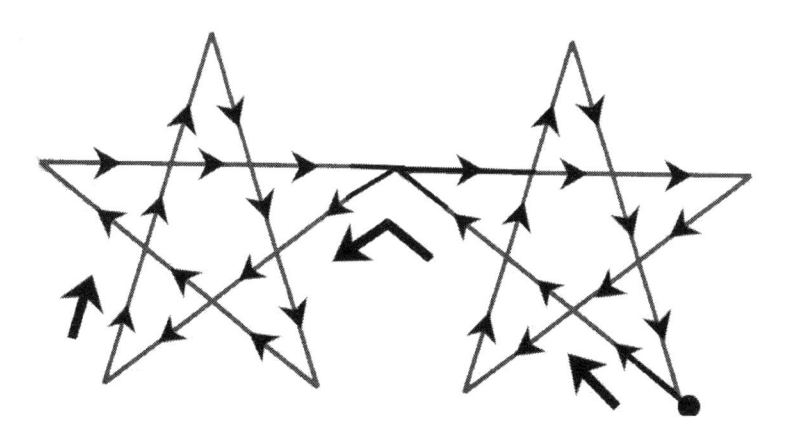

NAHAWAH KABIH OHAN DIATH SHIIBHA NOIIBHA BHAHAN

- Draw the portal clockwise and leave the south side of the portal open.

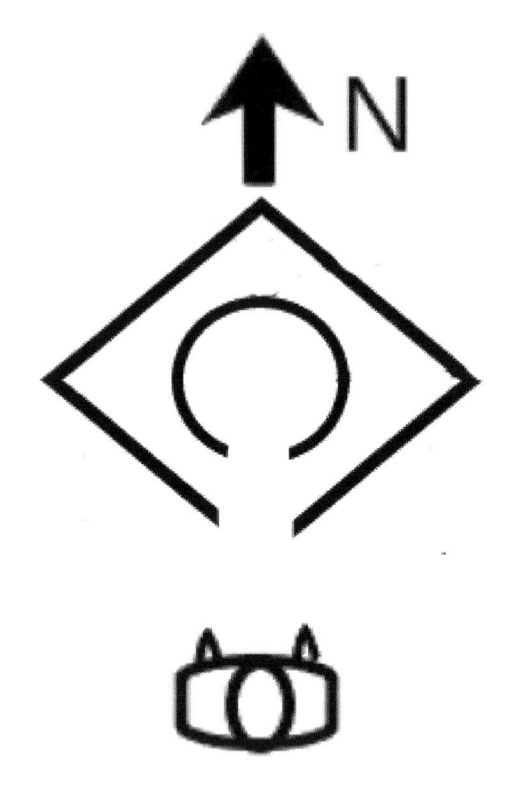

- Place the **CRAVO** incense in the center of the circle and a **WHITE** or **BLACK** candle inside the external design at the north end. Then light them up.
- Finish the drawing by closing the portal.

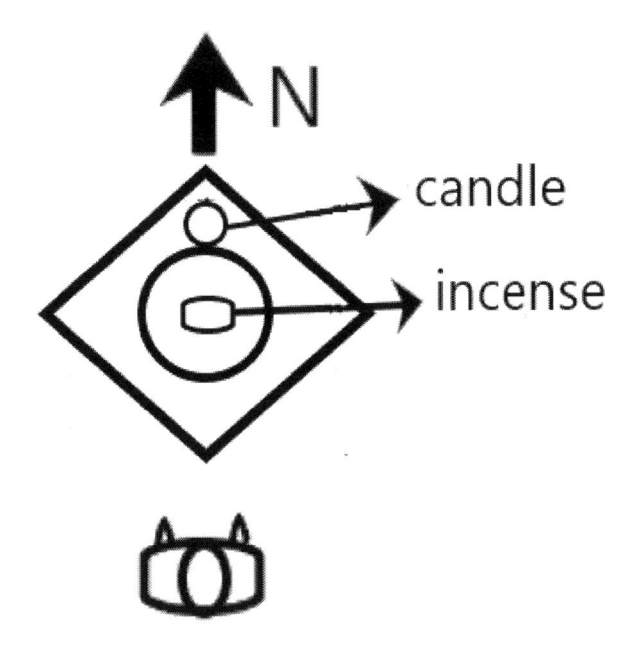

- Turn off the light.

- Standing with your hands at your sides, recite the invitation:

"THANIBHA HUABHI SHIAN NANABHI HASHIBHU"

- Wait a few seconds in silence.

- ➤ Draw the key in the air in front of the portal.

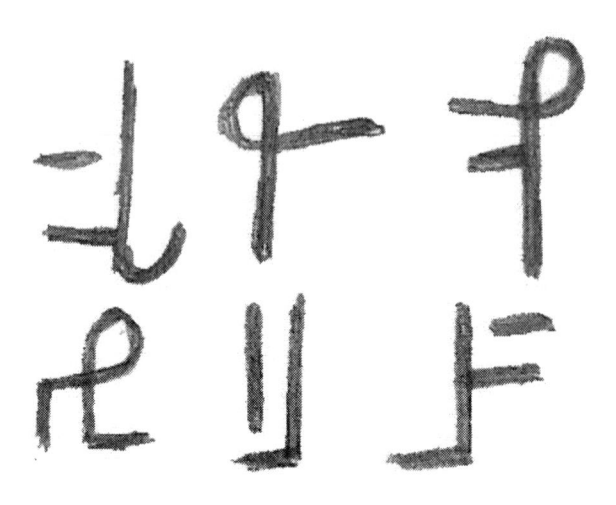

- ➤ Wait a few seconds.
- ➤ Now recite the evocation 3 times:

"KIU TANBHERINI NARANA RIUNA KASHID KORANA MANDARAH"

- ➤ Wait a few minutes and if you do not feel the presence of Tanbherini repeat the above evocation 3 more times.
- ➤ Wait a few minutes.

- If Tanbherini has not yet manifested himself, recite the second evocation 3 times.

"TANBHERINI RIUNA NOAN TIBHARA BHABOM"

- At the end of the third recitation it will be there, whether you feel it or not.
- Throw the piece of paper with your order into the portal. You can write the order on paper before or at that moment of the ritual, in the presence of Tanbherini.
- Mentalize the order for a minimum of 5 minutes, imagine your order being fulfilled, feel the emotion.
- After you have mentalized, say:

"I am grateful to Tanbherini for having heard my call and I am grateful for the request made"

- End the ritual.
- Trace the double pentagram in the air and at the same time vibrate the words of power:

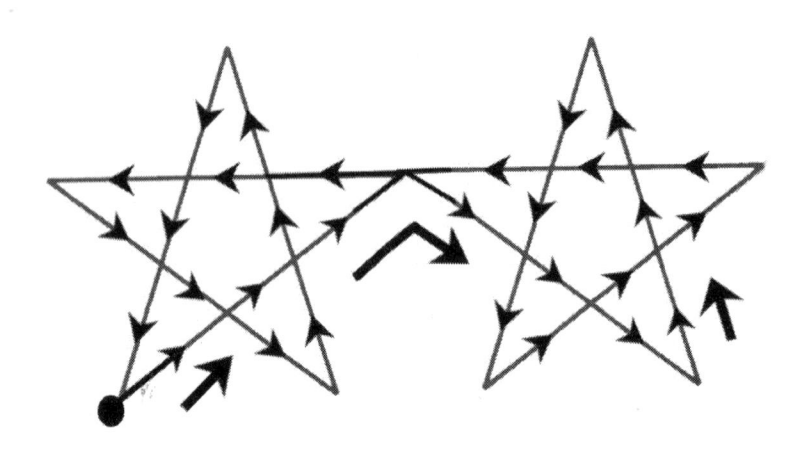

NAHAWAI NOHONAI NAMAHA NAMENIHI KOAN BHALIHI

- Exit the room and let the candle and incense burn to the end.
- Come back 24 hours later to clean up.
- Go back to your normal routine and wait for the results of the ritual without anxiety or doubt.

Dhithupo

SPECIALTIES

- Make financial profit through intelligence.

- Achieve good grades in tests and exams.
- Distort the facts in your favor.
- Get houses and land.
- Manipulating someone else's will to your advantage.

GOETIA

- Corresponds to Dantalion.

RITUAL

- To the north.
- Trace the double pentagram in the air and at the same time vibrate the words of power:

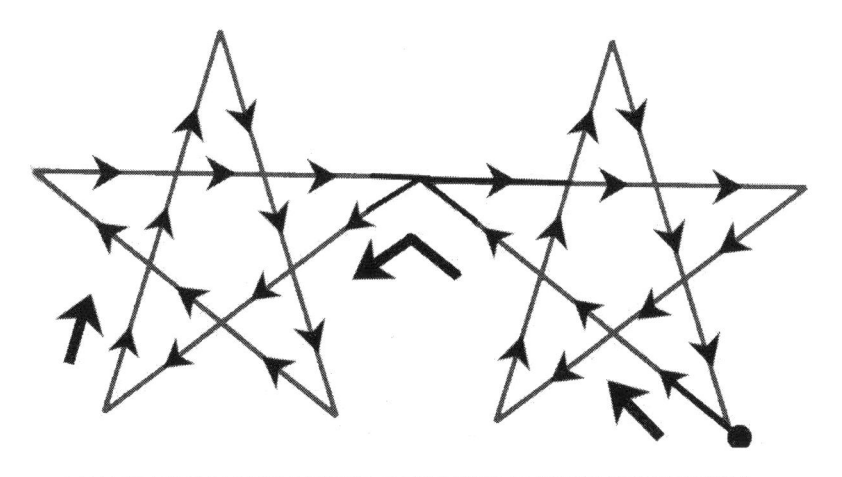

NAHAWAH KABIH OHAN DIATH SHIIBHA NOIIBHA BHAHAN

> Draw the portal clockwise and leave the south side of the portal open.

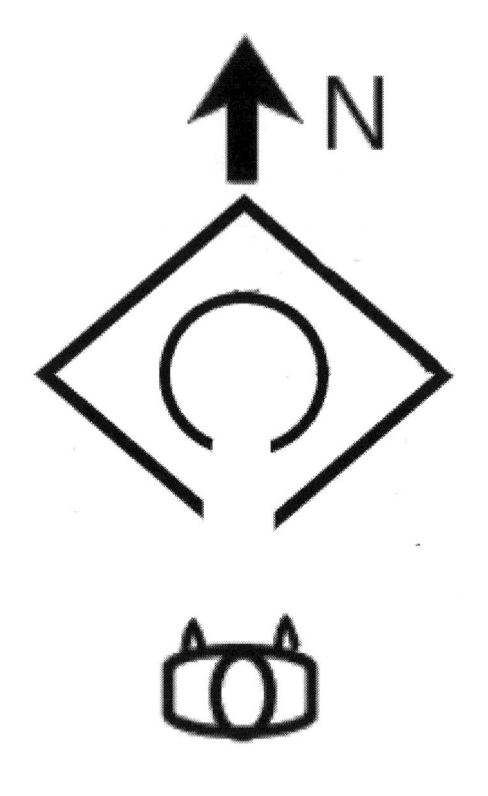

- ➢ Place the **DRAGON BLOOD** incense in the center of the circle and a **BLACK** candle inside the square at the north end. Then light them.
- ➢ Finish the drawing by closing the portal.

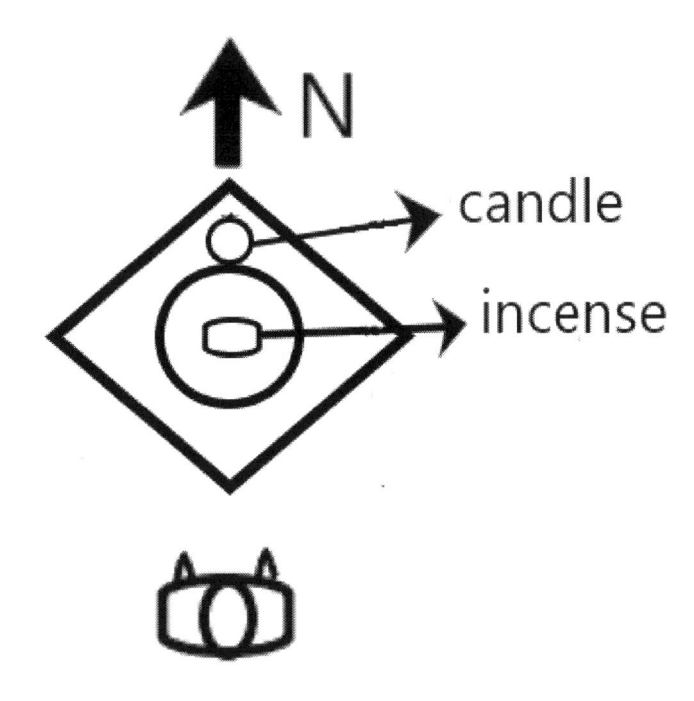

- Turn off the light.

- Standing with your hands close to your body, recite the invitation:

"KANIBHA KASHID THANIBHA HUABHI SHORANA NANABHI"

➢ Wait a few seconds in silence.

➢ Draw the key in the air in front of the portal.

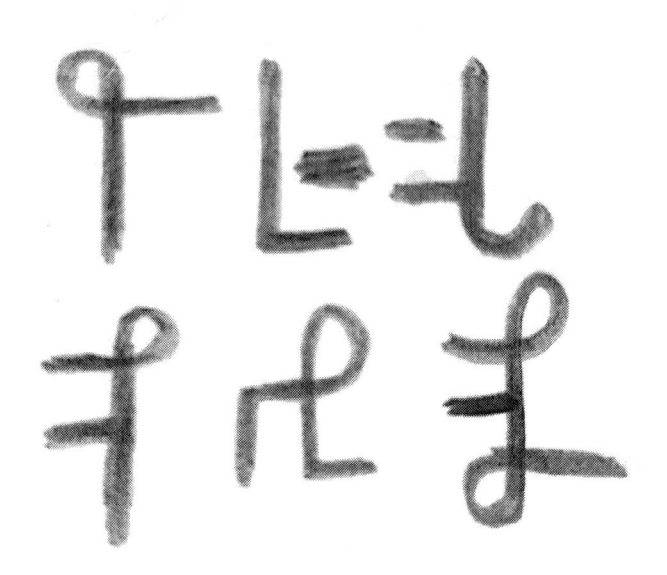

➢ Wait a few seconds.

➢ Now recite the evocation 3 times:

"KANIBHA KARANA DHITHUPO RIUNA PAMDARAH"

- Wait a few minutes and if you don't feel Dhithupo's presence repeat the above evocation 3 more times.
- Wait a few minutes.

- If Dhithupo has not yet manifested, recite the second evocation 3 times.

"KANIBHA DHITHUPO RIUNA KOAN NAGARA SHORANA"

- At the end of the third recitation it will be there, whether you feel it or not.
- Throw the piece of paper with your order inside the portal. You can write the request on paper before or at this time of the ritual, in Dhithupo's presence.
- Mind the request for at least 5 minutes, imagine your request being carried out, feel the emotion.
- After having mentalized, say:

"I thank Dhithupo for having listened to my call and I thank him for the request made."

- End the ritual.
- Trace the double pentagram in the air and at the same time vibrate the words of power:

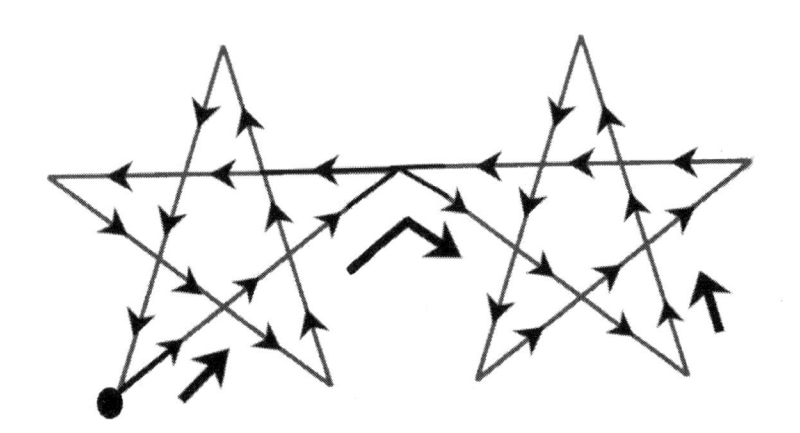

NAHAWAI NOHONAI NAMAHA NAMENIHI KOAN BHALIHI

- Leave the room and let the candle and incense burn to the end.
- Come back 24 hours later to clean everything up.
- Get back to your normal routine and wait for the results of the ritual without anxiety or doubt.

Garina

SPECIALTIES

- ➢ Increased wisdom.
- ➢ Good fame and abundance.
- ➢ Increase awareness.
- ➢ Increase in assets and possessions.
- ➢ Speak in a magnetic way.
- ➢ Cause the enemy pain and suffering.
- ➢ Cause the enemy a painful illness.

GOETIA

- ➢ Corresponds to Agares.

RITUAL

- ➢ To the north.
- ➢ Trace the double pentagram in the air and at the same time vibrate the words of power:

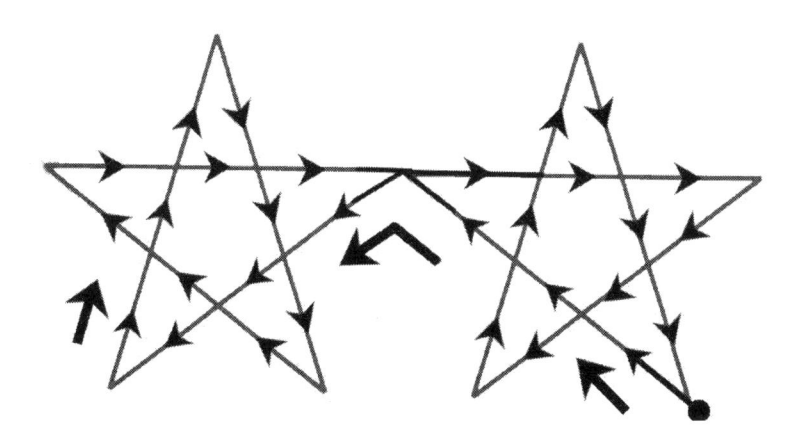

NAHAWAH KABIH OHAN DIATH SHIIBHA NOIIBHA BHAHAN

➢ Draw the portal clockwise and leave the south side of the portal open.

➢ Place the **CRAVO** incense in the center of the circle and a **WHITE** or **RED** candle inside the external design at the north end. Then light them up.
➢ Finish the drawing by closing the portal

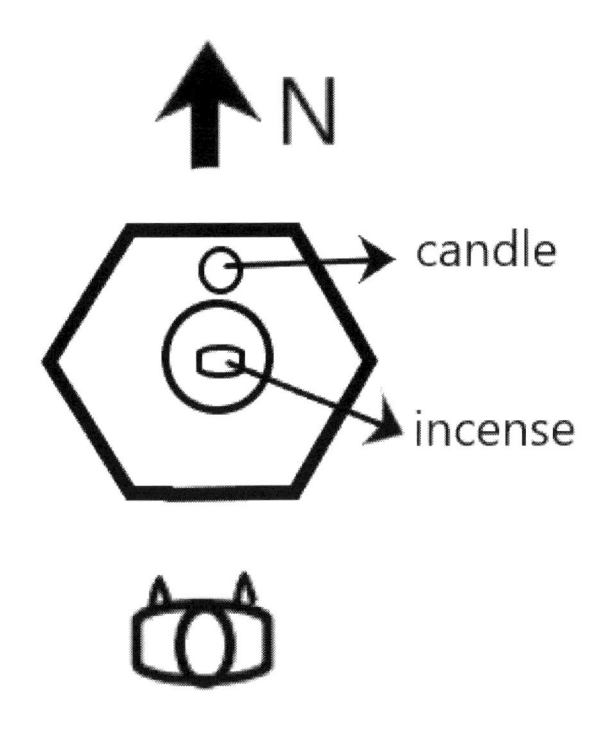

- Turn off the light.
- Standing with your hands at your sides, recite the invitation:

"THABHAO SHIAN HUANI SHABHI SHIABH"

- Wait a few seconds in silence.

➢ Draw the key in the air in front of the portal.

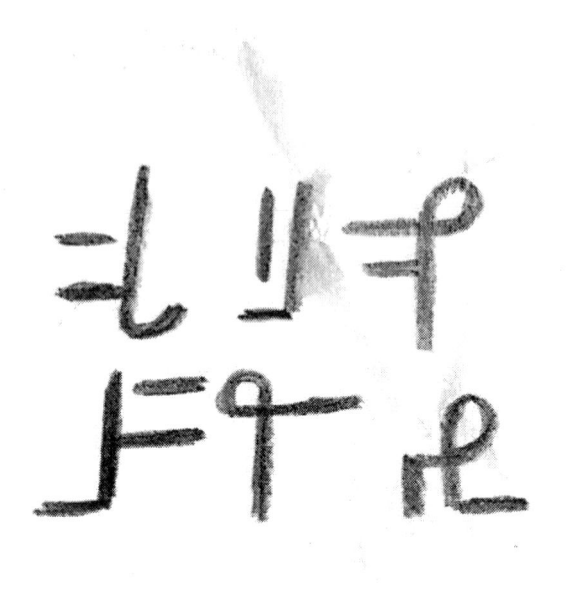

➢ Wait a few seconds.

➢ Now recite the evocation 3 times:

"HUANI GARINA NAKAN PAPARA BHOAN"

➢ Wait a few minutes and if you do not feel the presence of Garina repeat the above evocation 3 more times.

- Wait a few minutes.
- If Garina has not yet spoken, recite the second evocation 3 times.

"PAPARA BHOAN RIUNA KOAN TIBHARA GARINA OMAN"

- At the end of the third recitation it will be there, whether you feel it or not.
- Throw the piece of paper with your order into the portal. You can write the order on paper before or at that moment of the ritual, in the presence of Garina.
- Mentalize the order for a minimum of 5 minutes, imagine your order being fulfilled, feel the emotion.
- After you have mentalized, say:

"I thank Garina for having heard my call and thank for the request."

- End the ritual.
- Trace the double pentagram in the air and at the same time vibrate the words of power:

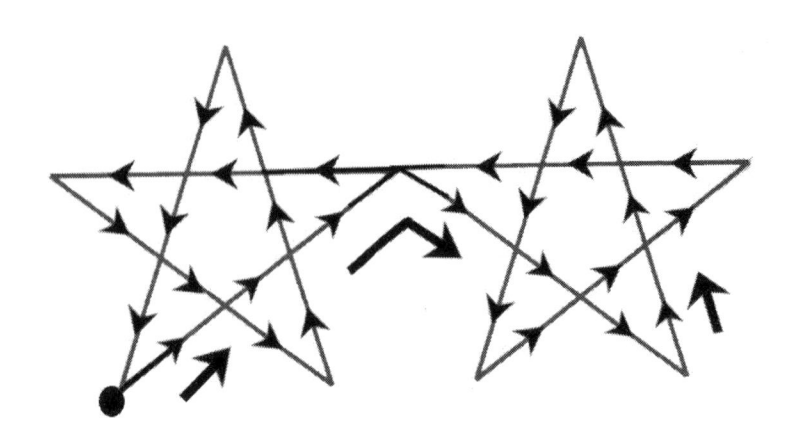

NAHAWAI NOHONAI NAMAHA NAMENIHI KOAN BHALIHI

- Exit the room and let the candle and incense burn to the end.
- Come back 24 hours later to clean up.
- Go back to your normal routine and wait for the results of the ritual without anxiety or doubt.

Dirindho

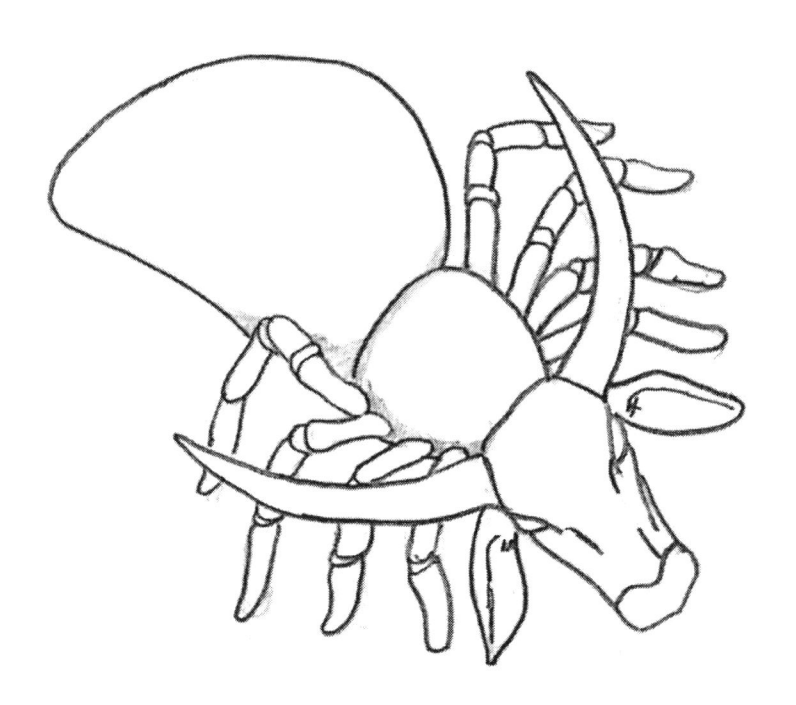

SPECIALTIES

- Win in lawsuit.
- Bring prosperity.
- Get wealth flow.

- ➢ Get specific amount of money.
- ➢ Subdue your enemy to you.
- ➢ Drive enemy mad.
- ➢ Making enemies take financial losses.

GOETIA

- ➢ It corresponds to Haagenti.

RITUAL

- ➢ To the north.
- ➢ Trace the double pentagram in the air and at the same time vibrate the words of power:

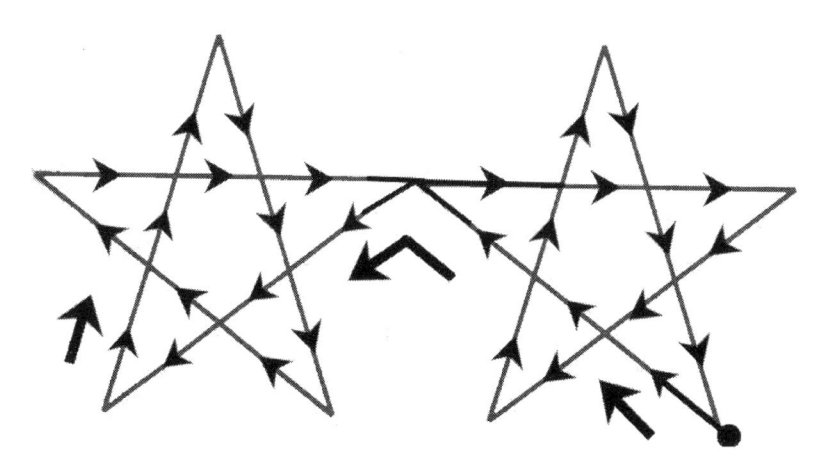

**NAHAWAH KABIH OHAN DIATH SHIIBHA
NOIIBHA BHAHAN**

➢ Draw the portal clockwise and leave the south side of the portal open.

- Place **CARNATION** or **JASMINE** incense in the center of the circle and a **WHITE** or **PURPLE** candle inside the design at the north end. Then light them.
- Finish the drawing by closing the portal.

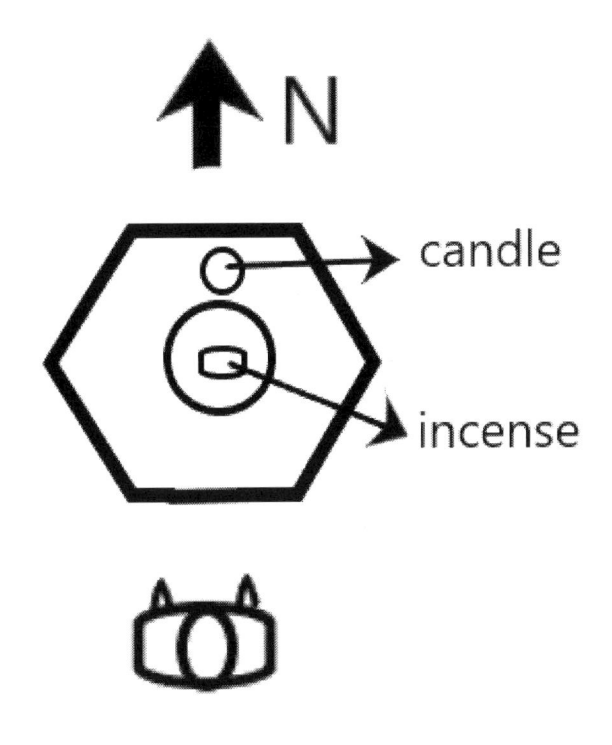

- ➢ Turn off the light.

- ➢ Standing with your hands close to your body, recite the invitation:

"KAPABHA THANIR HUABHI ABHAU SHIBHURA BANIBHU"

- ➢ Wait a few seconds in silence.

➢ Draw the key in the air in front of the portal.

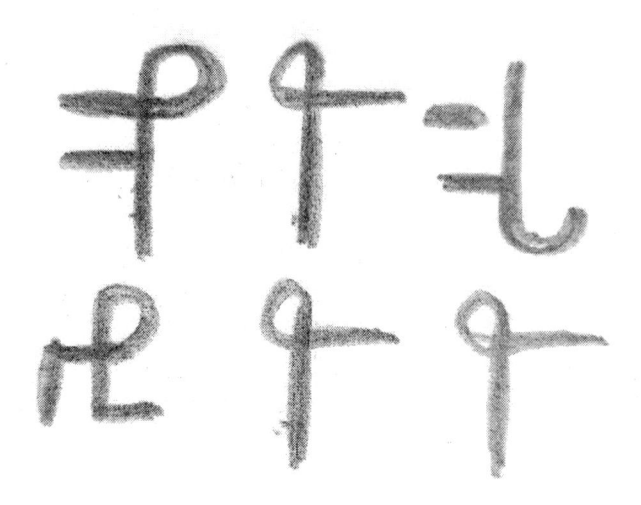

➢ Wait a few seconds.

➢ Now recite the evocation 3 times:

"KIV DIRINDHO KARANA BHIASH SHORANA NALI"

- Wait a few minutes and if you don't feel Dirindho's presence repeat the above evocation 3 more times.
- Wait a few minutes.

- If Dirindho has not yet manifested, recite the second evocation 3 times.

"DIRINDHO KOAN HASHARA NAGARA"

- At the end of the third recitation it will be there, whether you feel it or not.
- Throw the piece of paper with your order inside the portal. You can write the request on paper before or at this time of the ritual, in Dirindho's presence.
- Mind the request for at least 5 minutes, imagine your request being carried out, feel the emotion.
- After having mentalized, say:

"I thank Dirindho for having heard my call and I thank him for the request made."

- End the ritual.
- Trace the double pentagram in the air and at the same time vibrate the words of power:

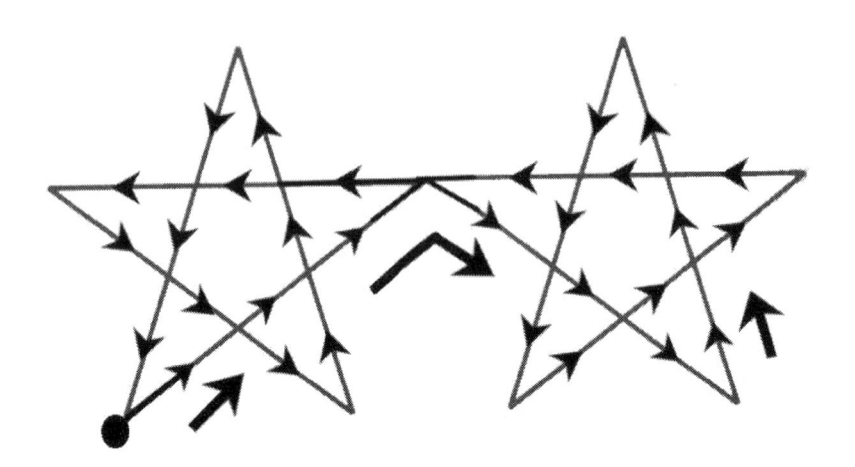

NAHAWAI NOHONAI NAMAHA NAMENIHI KOAN BHALIHI

- Leave the room and let the candle and incense burn to the end.
- Come back 24 hours later to clean everything up.
- Get back to your normal routine and wait for the results of the ritual without anxiety or doubt.

Makhisth

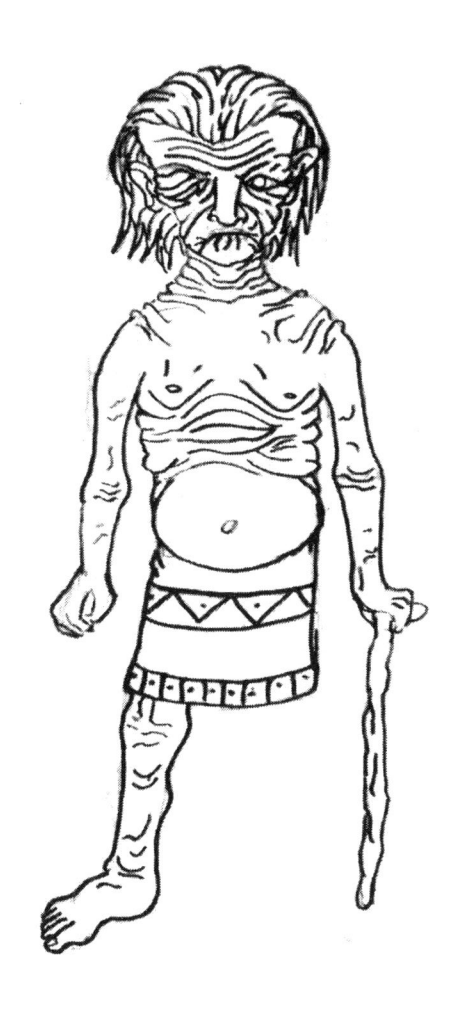

SPECIALTIES

- Generate unexpected wealth.
- Create wealth from scratch.
- Cause mental confusion in an enemy.
- Cause slow and violent enemy death.
- Cause terminal illness in an enemy.
- Induce your enemy to hang himself.
- Cause wounds to the enemy's entire body.

GOETIA

- Corresponds to Zagan.

RITUAL

- To the north.
- Trace the double pentagram in the air and at the same time vibrate the words of power:

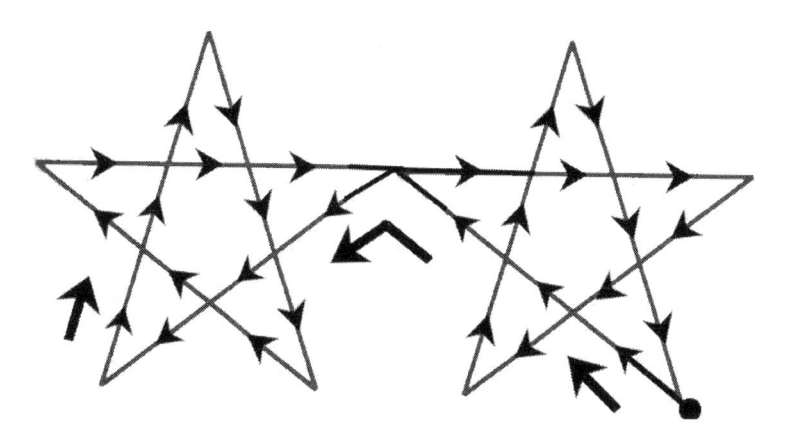

**NAHAWAH KABIH OHAN DIATH SHIIBHA
NOIIBHA BHAHAN**

> Draw the portal clockwise and leave the south side of the portal open.

- ➤ Place the **SAGE** incense in the center of the circle and a **WHITE** or **YELLOW** candle inside the outer design at the north end. Then light them up.
- ➤ Finish the drawing by closing the portal.

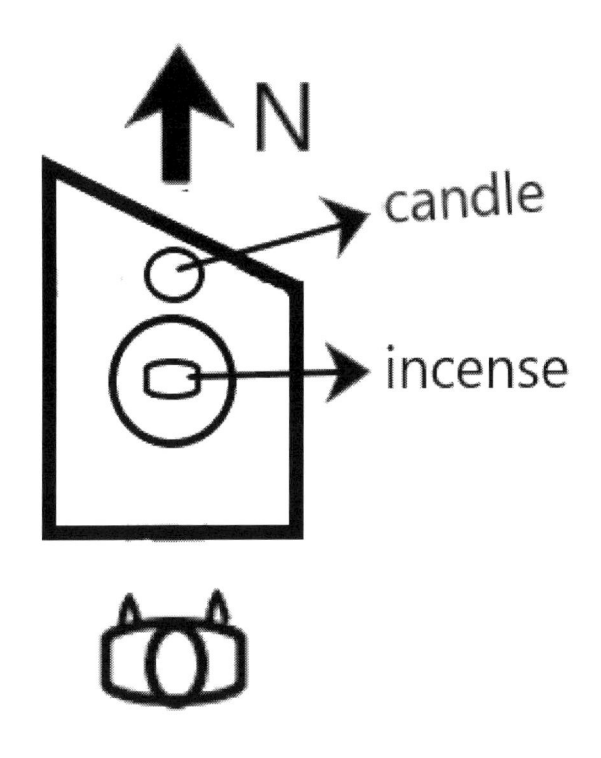

- Turn off the light.
- Standing with your hands at your sides, recite the invitation:

"BHIASH HUANI SHIAN SHANABHI BHIASH"

- ➢ Wait a few seconds in silence.
- ➢ Draw the key in the air in front of the portal.

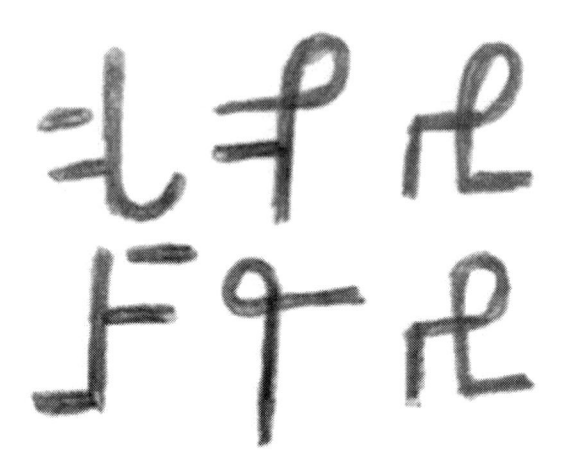

- ➢ Wait a few seconds.
- ➢ Now recite the evocation 3 times:

"KIU MAKHISTHIA PORAN RIUNA KOAN PARARAH"

- ➢ Wait a few minutes and if you do not feel the presence of Makhisth repeat the above evocation 3 more times.
- ➢ Wait a few minutes.

- If Makhisth has not yet manifested himself, recite the second evocation 3 times.

"MAKHISTHIA RIUNA KOAN TIBHARA MAKHISTHIA PORAN"

- At the end of the third recitation it will be there, whether you feel it or not.
- Throw the piece of paper with your order into the portal. You can write the request on paper before or at that time of the ritual, in the presence of Makhisth.
- Mentalize the order for a minimum of 5 minutes, imagine your order being fulfilled, feel the emotion.
- After you have mentalized, say:

"I am grateful to Makhisth Nara for having heard my call and I am grateful for the request made."

- End the ritual.
- Trace the double pentagram in the air and at the same time vibrate the words of power:

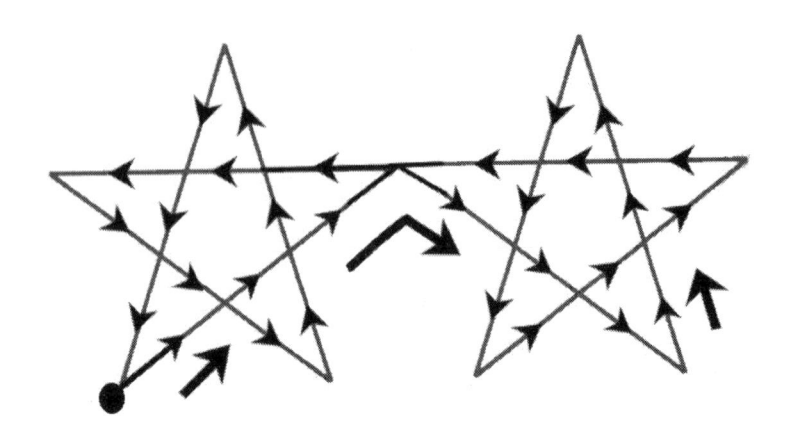

NAHAWAI NOHONAI NAMAHA NAMENIHI KOAN BHALIHI

- Exit the room and let the candle and incense burn to the end.
- Come back 24 hours later to clean up.
- Go back to your normal routine and wait for the results of the ritual without anxiety or doubt.

Hifh

SPECIALTIES

- Increase physical stamina.
- Increase intelligence.
- Get great physical strength.
- Always be ahead of enemies.
- Cure disease.

- Inflict wounds on the enemy's body.
- Cause various diseases in enemy or group of enemies.

GOETIA

- It corresponds to Valefor.

RITUAL

- To the north.
- Trace the double pentagram in the air and at the same time vibrate the words of power:

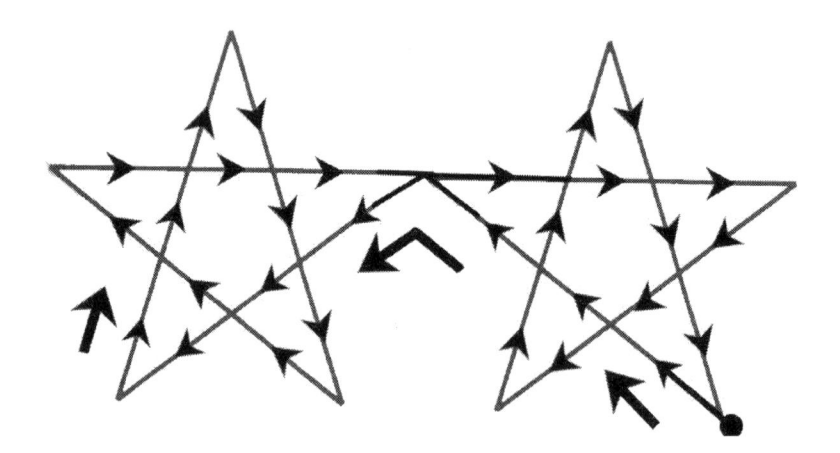

NAHAWAH KABIH OHAN DIATH SHIIBHA NOIIBHA BHAHAN

> ➤ Draw the portal clockwise and leave the south side of the portal open.

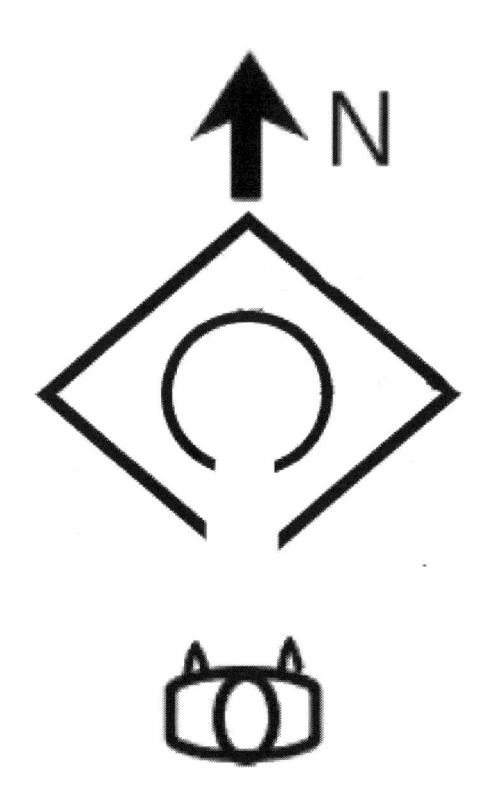

➢ Place the **ROSES** incense in the center of the circle and a **WHITE** or **BLACK** candle inside the design at the north end. Then light them.

➢ Finish the drawing by closing the portal.

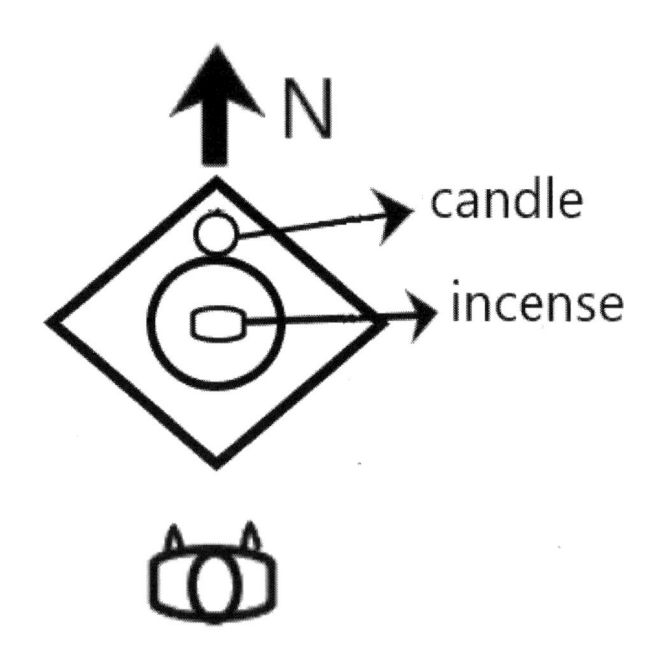

➢ Turn off the light.

➢ Standing with your hands close to your body, recite the invitation:

"THANIBHA BHIASHI NANABHI HISHIH BANIBHU"

- ➢ Wait a few seconds in silence.

- ➢ Draw the key in the air in front of the portal.

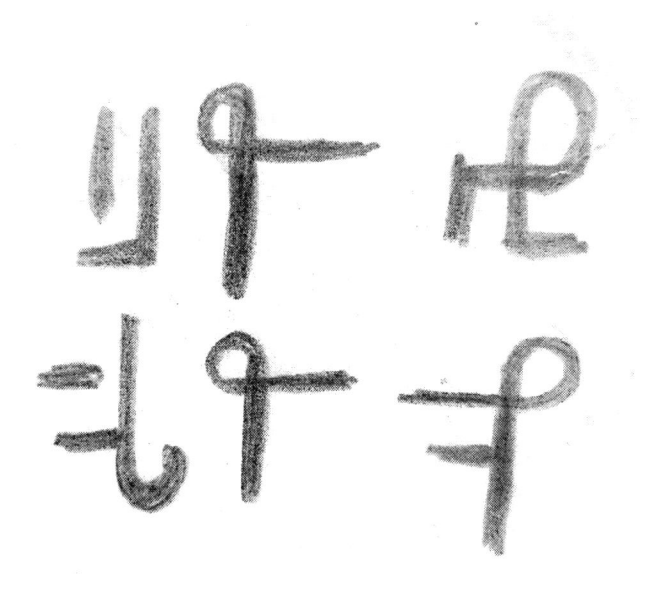

- ➢ Wait a few seconds.

- ➢ Now recite the evocation 3 times:

"PARAKA HIFH KARANA KOAN PAMDARAH NAMAHA"

- Wait a few minutes and if you don't feel the presence of Hifh repeat the above evocation 3 more times.
- Wait a few minutes.

- If Hifh has not yet manifested, recite the second evocation 3 times.

"HIFH KOGARA RIUNA KOAN NAGARA BOMHA"

- At the end of the third recitation it will be there, whether you feel it or not.
- Throw the piece of paper with your order inside the portal. You can write the request on paper before or at this time of the ritual, in the presence of Hifh.
- Mind the request for at least 5 minutes, imagine your request being carried out, feel the emotion.
- After having mentalized, say:

"I thank Hifh for having listened to my call and thank you for the request made."

- End the ritual.
- Trace the double pentagram in the air and at the same time vibrate the words of power:

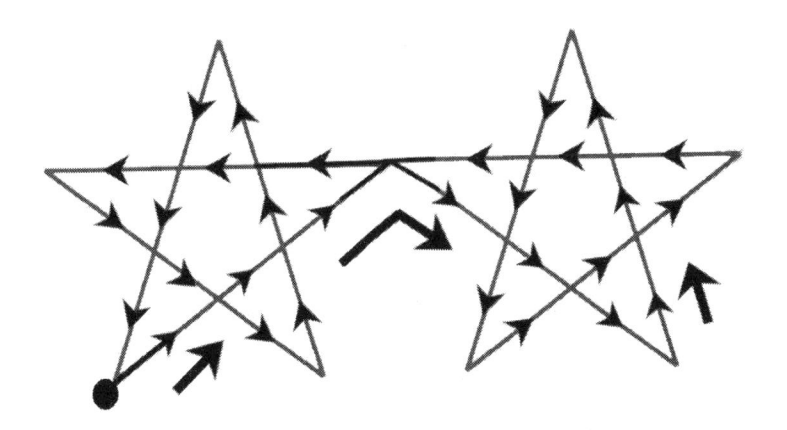

NAHAWAI NOHONAI NAMAHA NAMENIHI KOAN BHALIHI

- Leave the room and let the candle and incense burn to the end.
- Come back 24 hours later to clean everything up.

- Get back to your normal routine and wait for the results of the ritual without anxiety or doubt.

Paranga

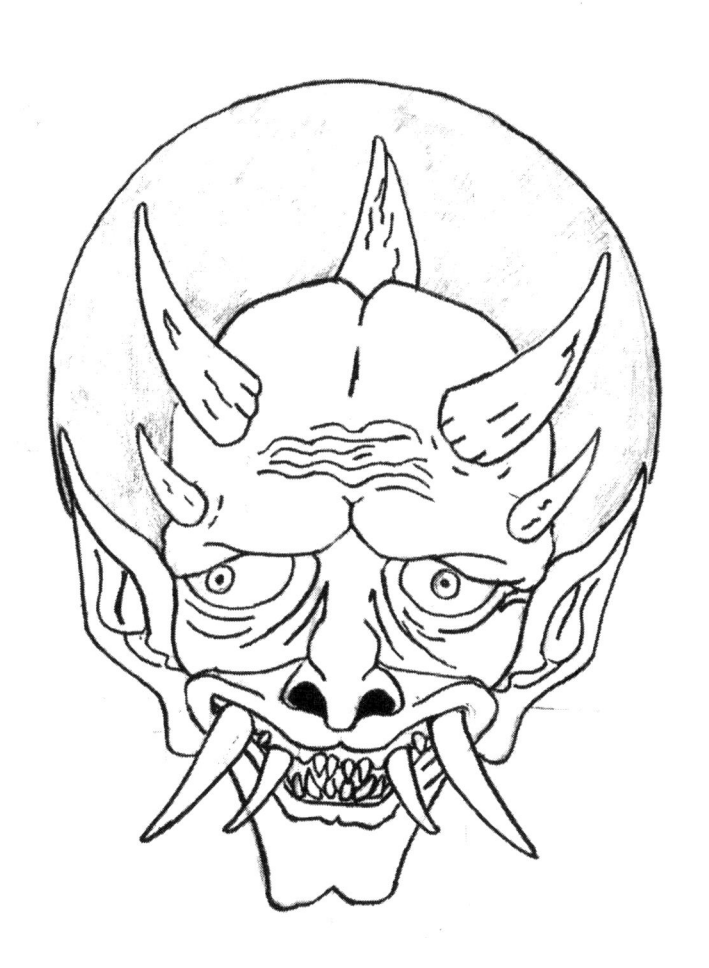

SPECIALTIES

- Cure diseases.
- Relieve pain.
- Cause disease.
- Promote an increase in physical vigor.
- Extend life.
- Cause sudden enemy death.
- Cause the enemy a painful death.
- Create hostility and hatred between other people and your enemy.

GOETIA

- Corresponds to Buer.

RITUAL

- To the north.
- Trace the double pentagram in the air and at the same time vibrate the words of power:

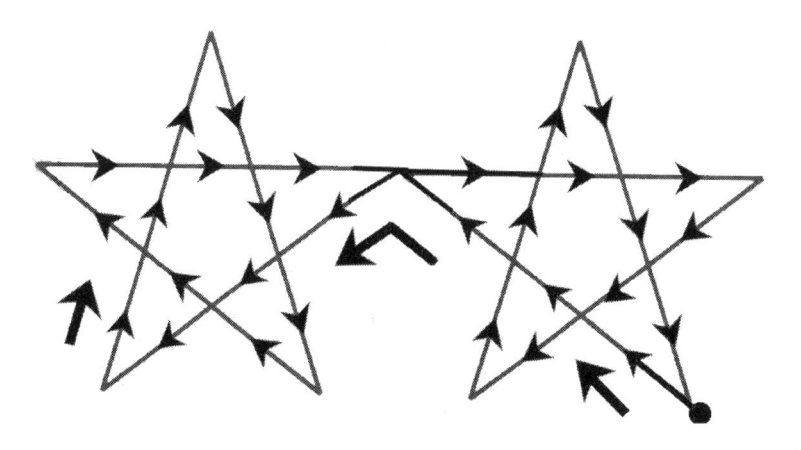

NAHAWAH KABIH OHAN DIATH SHIIBHA NOIIBHA BHAHAN

- Draw the portal clockwise and leave the south side of the portal open

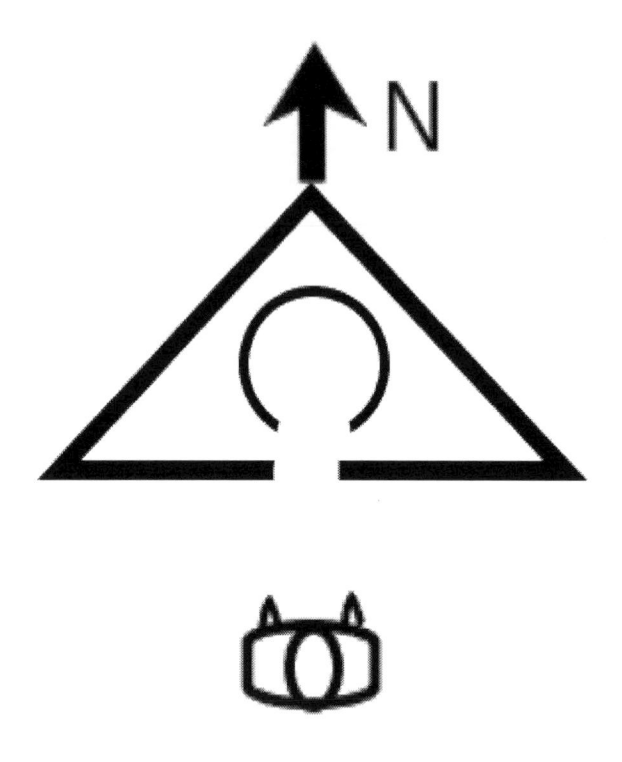

- ➤ Place **LAVENDER** incense in the center of the circle and a **WHITE** or **BLUE** candle inside the outer drawing at the north end. Then light them up.
- ➤ Finish the drawing by closing the portal.

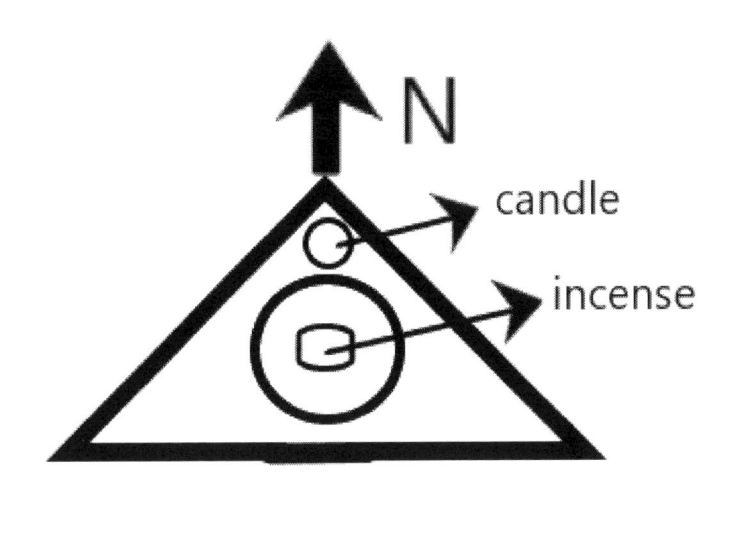

- ➤ Turn off the light.
- ➤ Standing with your hands at your sides, recite the invitation:

"THANIBHA HUANI SHIAN SHANABHI BHIASH"

- ➤ Wait a few seconds in silence.

➢ Draw the key in the air in front of the portal.

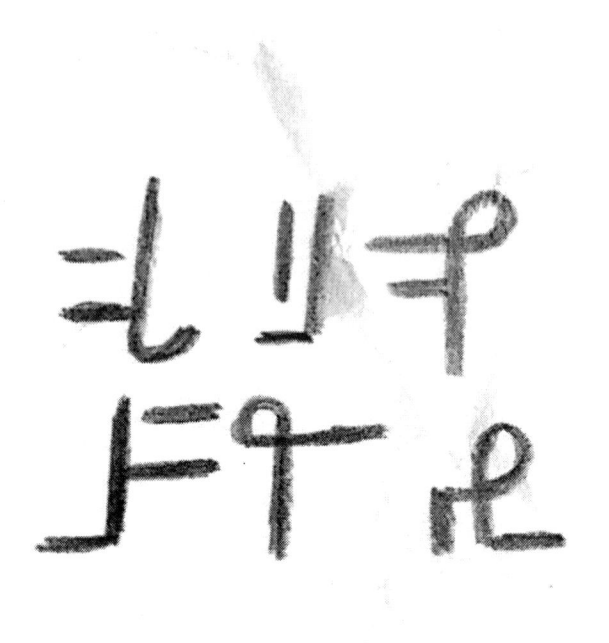

➢ Wait a few seconds.
➢ Now recite the evocation 3 times:

"KIU PARANGA NARA RIUNA PARANGA NARA KOAN"

➢ Wait a few minutes and if you do not feel the presence of Paranga, repeat the above evocation 3 more times.

- Wait a few minutes.
- If Paranga has not yet spoken, recite the second evocation 3 times:

"PARANGA NARA RIUNA KOAN TIBHARA PARANGA NARA"

- At the end of the third recitation it will be there, whether you feel it or not.
- Throw the piece of paper with your order into the portal. You can write the order on paper before or at that moment of the ritual, in the presence of Paranga.
- Mentalize the order for a minimum of 5 minutes, imagine your order being fulfilled, feel the emotion.
- After you have mentalized, say:

"I am grateful to Paranga Nara for having heard my call and I am grateful for the request made."

- End the ritual.
- Trace the double pentagram in the air and at the same time vibrate the words of power:

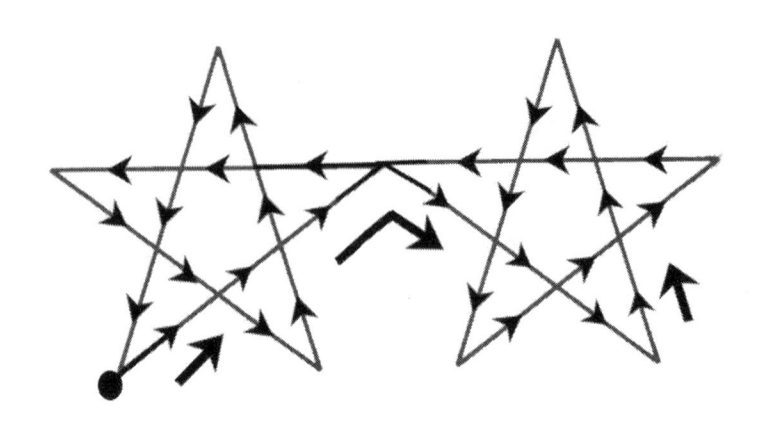

NAHAWAI NOHONAI NAMAHA NAMENIHI KOAN BHALIHI

- Exit the room and let the candle and incense burn to the end.
- Come back 24 hours later to clean up.
- Go back to your normal routine and wait for the results of the ritual without anxiety or doubt.

Shonzalorth

SPECIALTIES

- Become magnetic.
- Predict the future.

- Cause confusion and madness in an enemy.
- Increase the power of seduction.
- Persuasive speech.
- Increase convincing power.
- Change people's opinions.
- Cause the enemy to die by drowning.
- Lead enemies to misery.

GOETIA

- Corresponds to Amon.

RITUAL

- To the north.
- Trace the double pentagram in the air and at the same time vibrate the words of power:

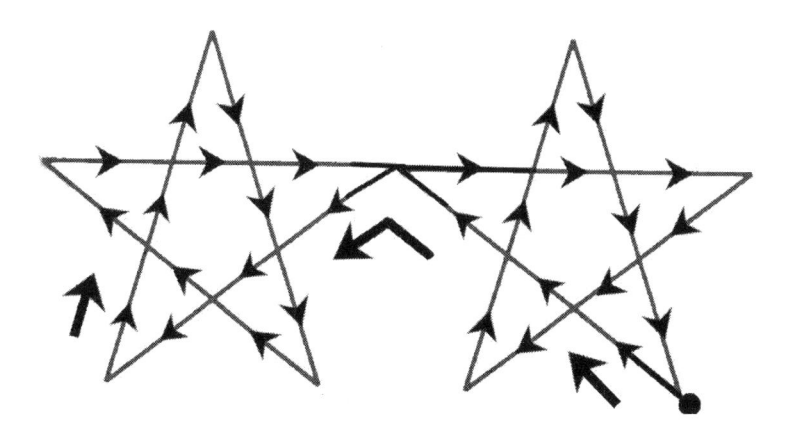

NAHAWAH KABIH OHAN DIATH SHIIBHA NOIIBHA BHAHAN

> Draw the portal clockwise and leave the south side of the portal open.

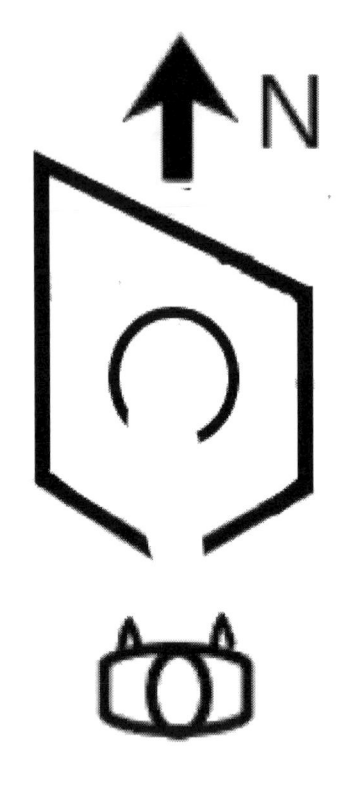

- Place **MIRRA** incense in the center of the circle and a **WHITE** or **RED** candle inside the outer design at the north end. Then light them up.
- Finish the drawing by closing the portal.

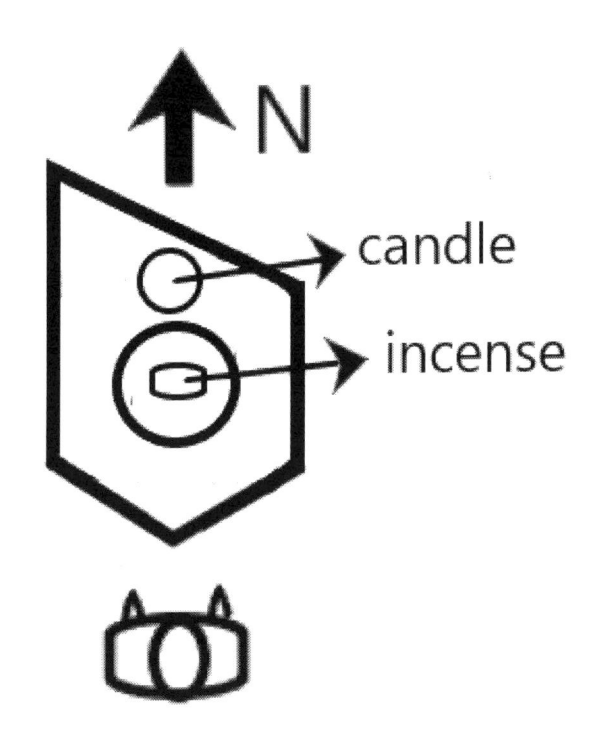

➢ Turn off the light.

➢ Standing with your hands at your sides, recite the invitation:

"THABHANI HUASH SHIAN SHANABHI KOAN"

- ➤ Wait a few seconds in silence.
- ➤ Draw the key in the air in front of the portal.

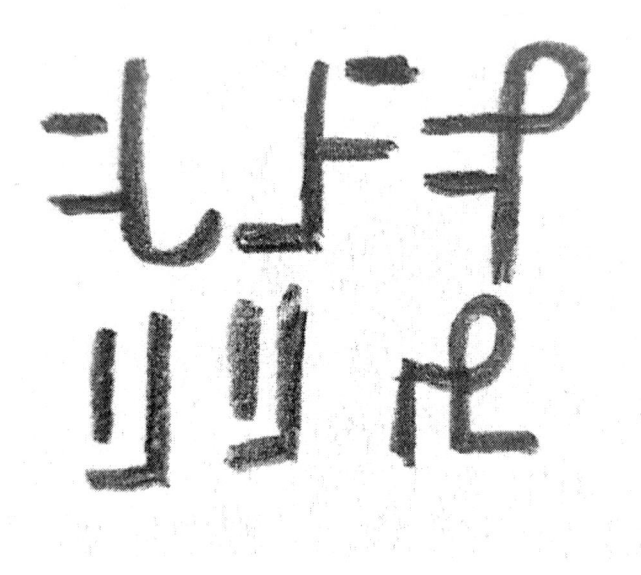

- ➤ Wait a few seconds.
- ➤ Now recite the evocation 3 times:

"PARASH PARASH SOLUHI NARA SHONZALORTH"

- ➤ Wait a few minutes and if you do not feel the presence of Shonzalorth repeat the above evocation 3 more times.

- Wait a few minutes.

- If Shonzalorth has not yet manifested, recite the second evocation 3 times.

"SHONZALORTH RIUNA KOAN TIBHARA SHIRIBHA"

- At the end of the third recitation it will be there, whether you feel it or not.
- Throw the piece of paper with your order into the portal. You can write the order on paper before or at that time of the ritual, in the presence of Shonzalorth.
- Mentalize the order for a minimum of 5 minutes, imagine your order being fulfilled, feel the emotion.
- After you have mentalized, say:

"I am grateful to Shonzalorth for having heard my call and I am grateful for the request made."

- End the ritual.

➢ Trace the double pentagram in the air and at the same time vibrate the words of power:

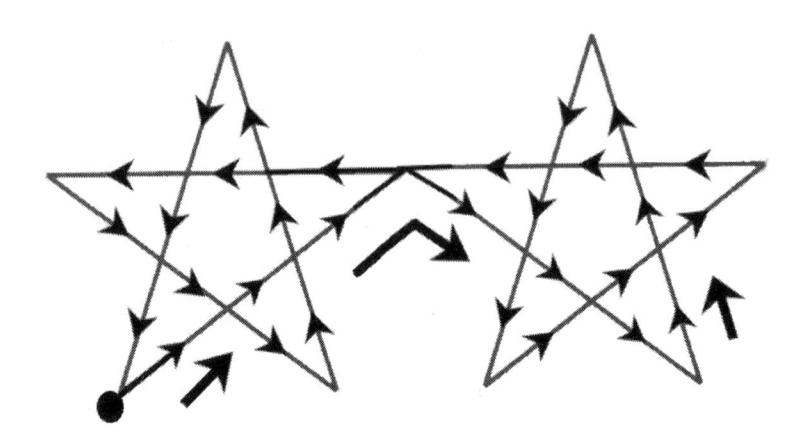

NAHAWAI NOHONAI NAMAHA NAMENIHI KOAN BHALIHI

➢ Exit the room and let the candle and incense burn to the end.
➢ Come back 24 hours later to clean up.
➢ Go back to your normal routine and wait for the results of the ritual without anxiety or doubt.

Poratha

SPECIALTIES

- ➢ Bringing fame and political power
- ➢ Generate profits through political influence
- ➢ Getting partners with large capital
- ➢ Create friendship between you and someone powerful

GOETIA

- ➢ It corresponds to Eligos.

RITUAL

- ➢ To the north.
- ➢ Trace the double pentagram in the air and at the same time vibrate the words of power:

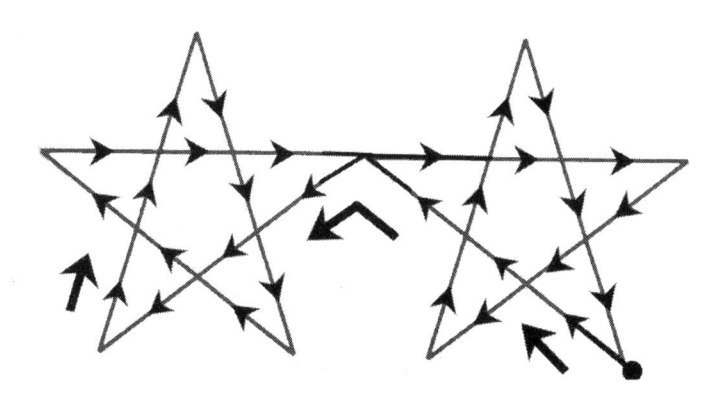

NAHAWAH KABIH OHAN DIATH SHIIBHA NOIIBHA BHAHAN

> ➢ Draw the portal clockwise and leave the south side of the portal open.

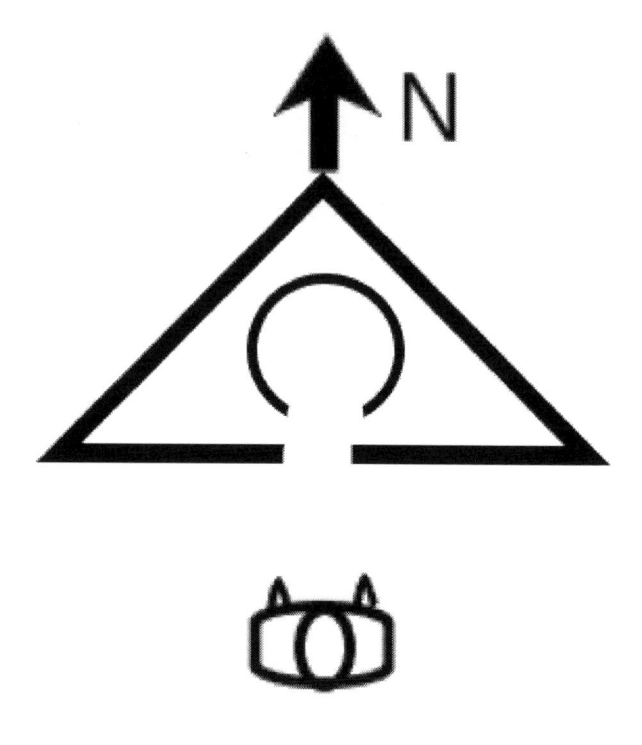

- ➢ Place **CEDAR** incense in the center of the circle and a **BLACK** candle inside the portal at the north end. Then light them.
- ➢ Finish the drawing by closing the portal.

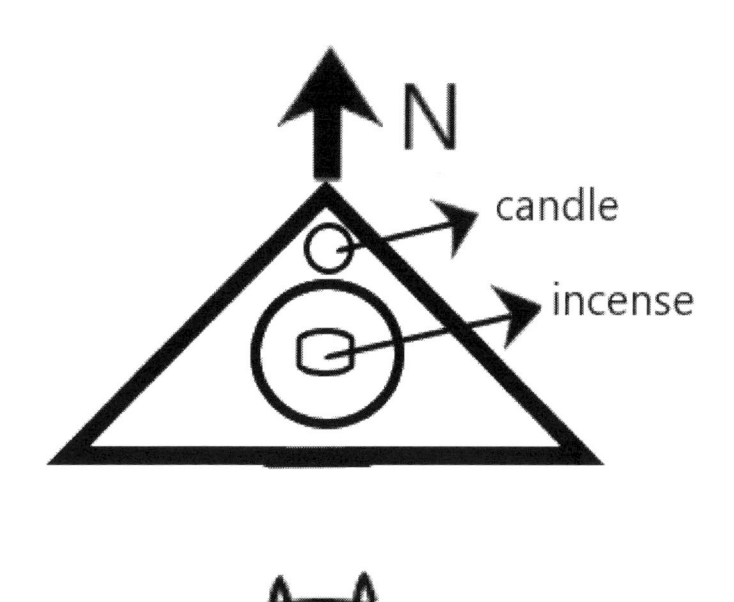

➢ Turn off the light.

➢ Pierce your finger and place 1 drop of blood inside the inner circle
➢ wait a few seconds

- ➢ Standing with your hands close to your body, recite the invitation:

"KANIBHA BANIBHU THANIBHA HUABHI NANABHI HASHIBHU"

- ➢ Wait a few seconds in silence.

- ➢ Draw the key in the air in front of the portal.

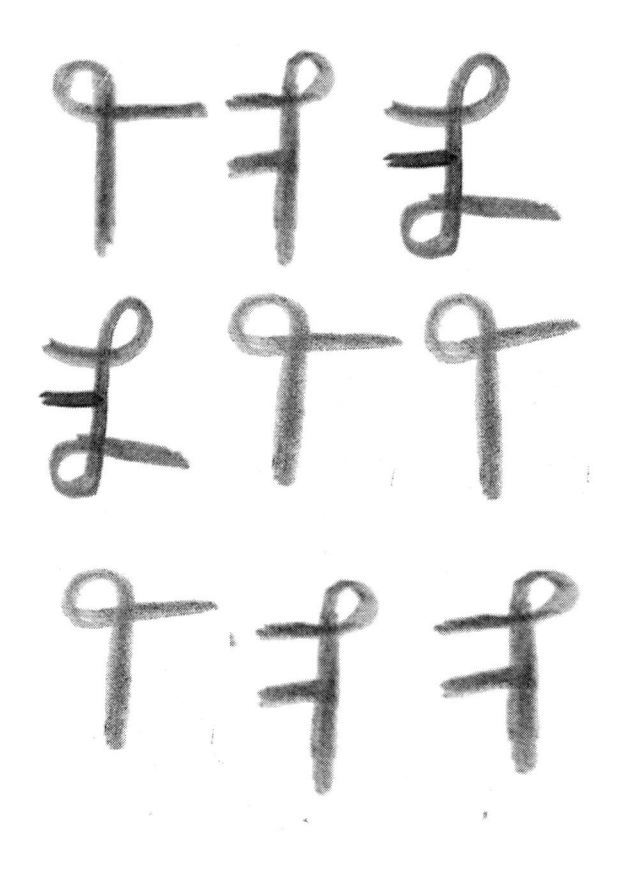

- Wait a few seconds.

- Now recite the evocation 3 times:

"PORATHA KANIBHA NAHAWAH KARANA RIUNA KASHID SHORANA"

- ➢ Wait a few minutes and if you don't feel Poratha's presence repeat the above evocation 3 more times.
- ➢ Wait a few minutes.

- ➢ If Poratha has not yet manifested, recite the second evocation 3 times.

"PORATHA KARANA KOAN NAGARA SHORANA"

- ➢ At the end of the third recitation it will be there, whether you feel it or not.
- ➢ Throw the piece of paper with your order inside the portal. You can write the request on paper before or at this time of the ritual, in Poratha's presence.
- ➢ Envision the request for at least 5 minutes, imagine your request taking place, feel the emotion.
- ➢ After having mentalized, say:

"I thank Poratha for having listened to my call and I thank him for the request made."

- End the ritual.
- Trace the double pentagram in the air and at the same time vibrate the words of power:

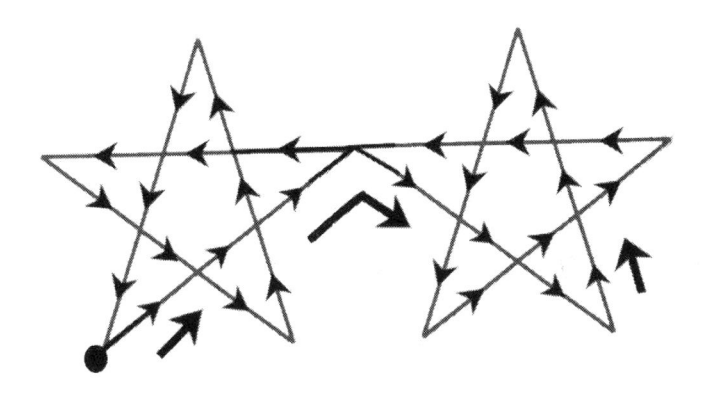

NAHAWAI NOHONAI NAMAHA NAMENIHI KOAN BHALIHI

- Leave the room and let the candle and incense burn to the end.
- Come back 24 hours later to clean everything up.
- Get back to your normal routine and wait for the results of the ritual without anxiety or doubt.

Onpahan

SPECIALTIES

- Loving union.
- Become magnetic.
- Convince large group.

- Increase the power of seduction.
- Persuasive speech.
- Political power.
- Increase convincing power.
- Change people's opinions.
- Set anyone against your enemy.
- Make the enemy lose credibility.

GOETIA

- Corresponds to Beleth.

RITUAL

- To the north.
- Trace the double pentagram in the air and at the same time vibrate the words of power:

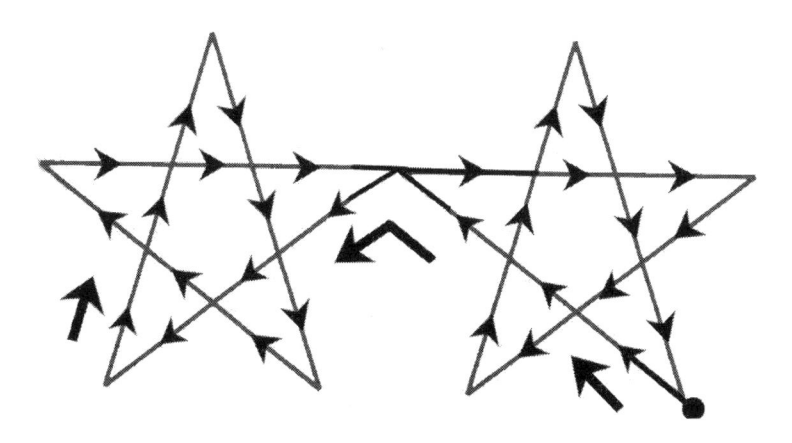

NAHAWAH KABIH OHAN DIATH SHIIBHA NOIIBHA BHAHAN

- ➢ Draw the portal clockwise and leave the south side of the portal open.

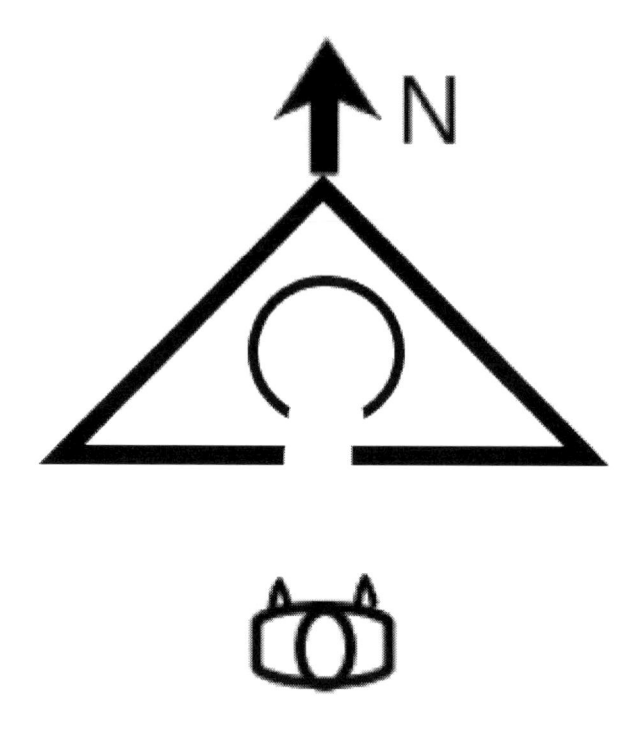

- ➢ Place the **JASMINE** incense in the center of the circle and a **WHITE** or **RED** candle inside the outer design at the north end. Then light them up.
- ➢ Finish the drawing by closing the portal.

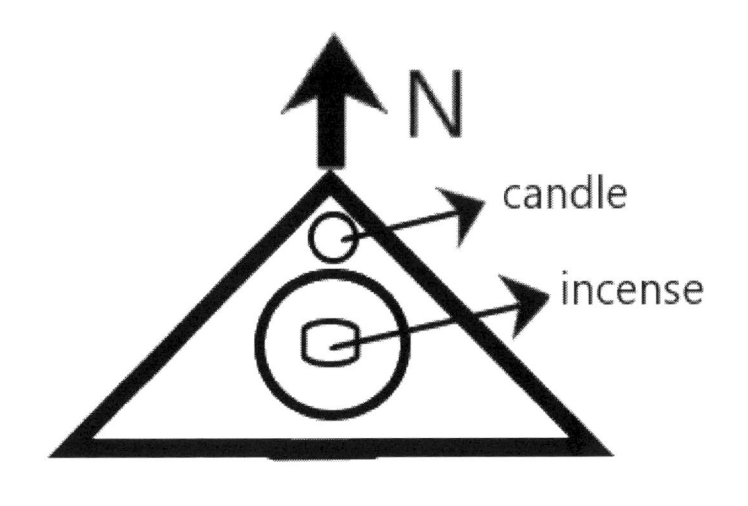

- Turn off the light.
- Standing with your hands at your sides, recite the invitation:

"NEBHIRA MANAK SHIAN SHANABHI KOAN"

- Wait a few seconds in silence.
- Draw the key in the air in front of the portal.

- ➢ Wait a few seconds.
- ➢ Now recite the evocation 3 times:

"ONPAHAN ARASH NEBHIRA PINURA HASHAN"

- ➢ Wait a few minutes and if you do not feel the presence of Onpahan repeat the above evocation 3 more times.
- ➢ Wait a few minutes.

- If Onpahan has not yet manifested, recite the second evocation 3 times.

"ONPAHAN ARASH NEBHIRA SHOHATHA HASHAN"

- At the end of the third recitation it will be there, whether you feel it or not.
- Throw the piece of paper with your order into the portal. You can write the order on paper before or at that time of the ritual, in the presence of Onpahan.
- Mentalize the order for a minimum of 5 minutes, imagine your order being fulfilled, feel the emotion.
- After you have mentalized, say:

"I am grateful to Onpahan for having heard my call and I am grateful for the request made."

- End the ritual.
- Trace the double pentagram in the air and at the same time vibrate the words of power:

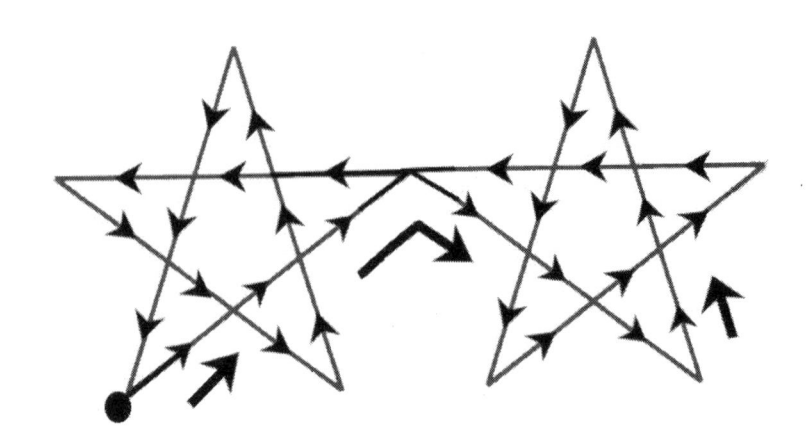

NAHAWAI NOHONAI NAMAHA NAMENIHI KOAN BHALIHI

- Exit the room and let the candle and incense burn to the end.
- Come back 24 hours later to clean up.
- Go back to your normal routine and wait for the results of the ritual without anxiety or doubt.

Halh

SPECIALTIES

- Produce wealth from nothing.
- Predict the future.
- Express money.

- Bring financial profit.
- Enable the enemy to carry out your orders.
- Bring financial loss to the enemy.
- Change people's opinions.

GOETIA

- Corresponds to Vassago.

RITUAL

- To the north.
- Trace the double pentagram in the air and at the same time vibrate the words of power:

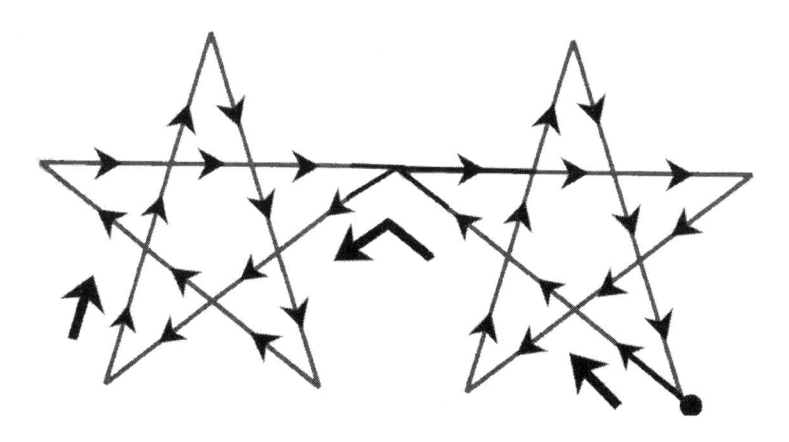

**NAHAWAH KABIH OHAN DIATH SHIIBHA
NOIIBHA BHAHAN**

> ➢ Draw the portal clockwise and leave the south side of the portal open.

- Place the **CRAVO** incense in the center of the circle and a **WHITE** or **GREEN** candle inside the external design at the north end. Then light them up.
- Finish the drawing by closing the portal.

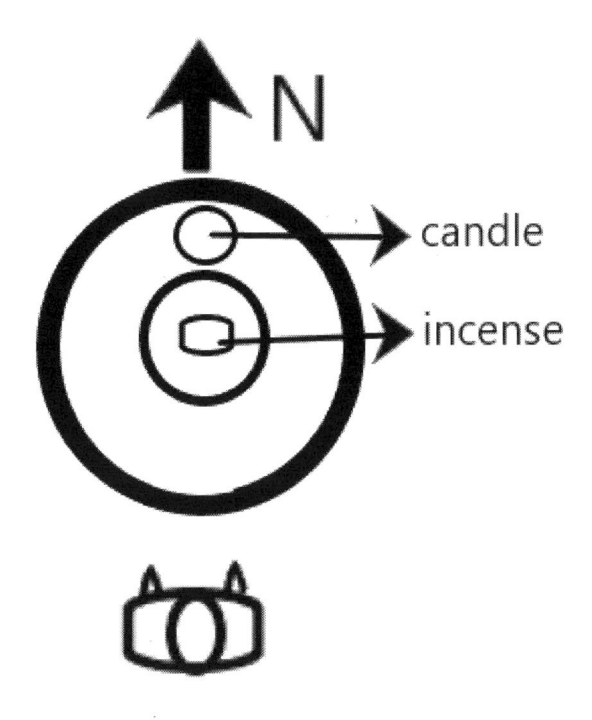

- Turn off the light.
- Standing with your hands at your sides, recite the invitation:

"THABHANI HUASH SHANABHI KOAN PARASH"

- Wait a few seconds in silence.
  Draw the key in the air in front of the portal

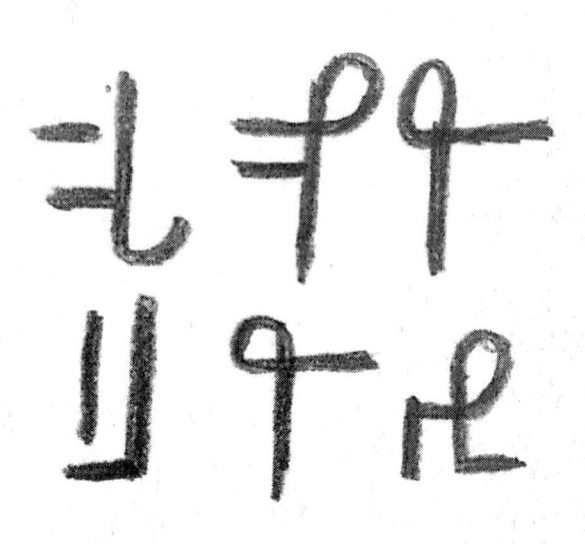

- ➤ Wait a few seconds.
- ➤ Now recite the evocation 3 times:

"AVENIS HALH SHIBHIRA PARASH RIUNA KANKARH"

- ➤ Wait a few minutes and if you do not feel the presence of Halh repeat the above evocation 3 more times.
- ➤ Wait a few minutes.

- If Halh has not yet manifested, recite the second evocation 3 times.

"AVENIS HALH RIUNA KOAN PARASH SHIRIBHA"

- At the end of the third recitation it will be there, whether you feel it or not.
- Throw the piece of paper with your order into the portal. You can write the order on paper before or at that time of the ritual, in Halh's presence.
- Mentalize the order for a minimum of 5 minutes, imagine your order being fulfilled, feel the emotion.
- After you have mentalized, say:

"I am grateful to Halh for having heard my call and I am grateful for the request made."

- End the ritual.
- Trace the double pentagram in the air and at the same time vibrate the words of power:

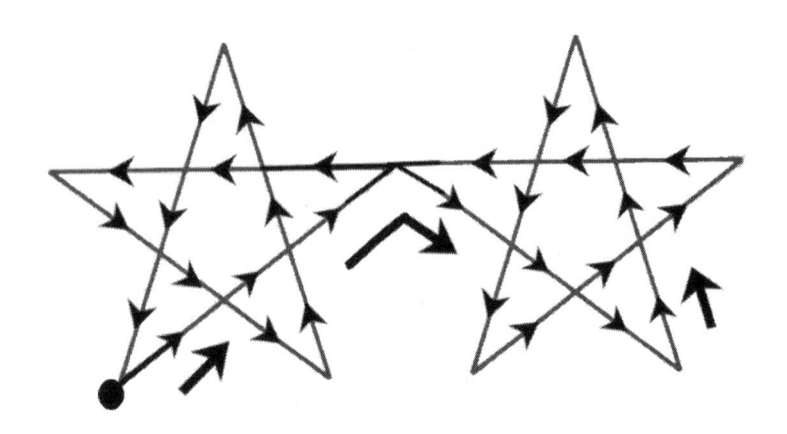

NAHAWAI NOHONAI NAMAHA NAMENIHI KOAN BHALIHI

- Exit the room and let the candle and incense burn to the end.
- Come back 24 hours later to clean up.
- Go back to your normal routine and wait for the results of the ritual without anxiety or doubt.

Vanoilth

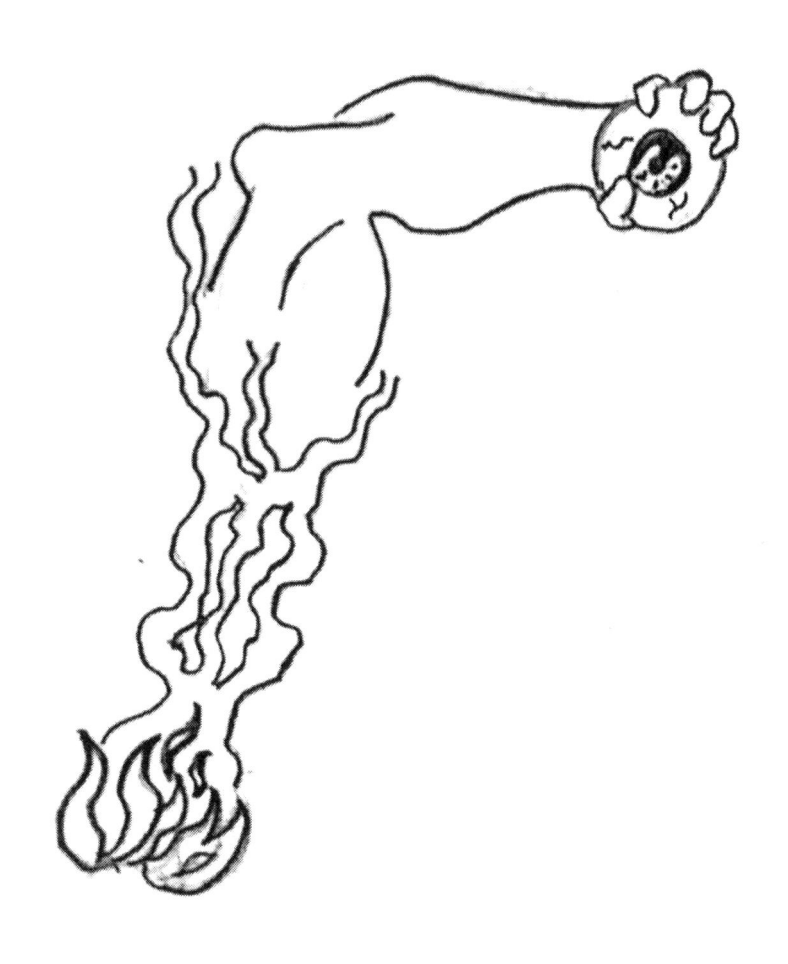

SPECIALTIES

- Bring money.
- Generate prosperity flow.
- Give power over enemies.
- Increase material goods.
- Discover traitor.
- Achieve goals faster.
- Cause the enemy to die by fire.

GOETIA

- Corresponds to Seere.

RITUAL

- To the north.
- Trace the double pentagram in the air and at the same time vibrate the words of power:

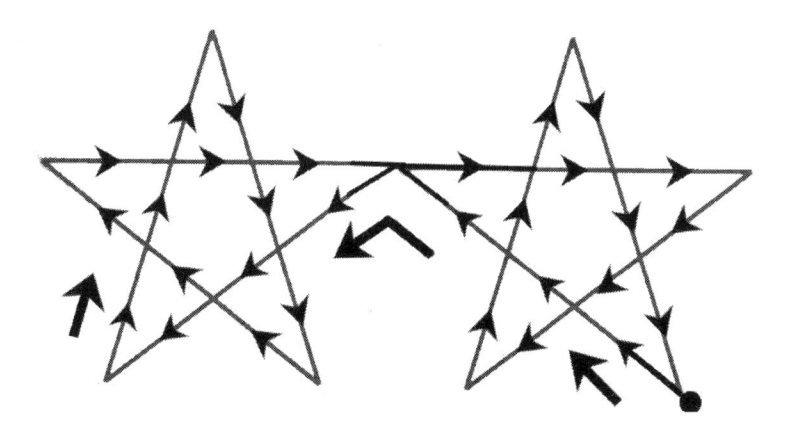

**NAHAWAH KABIH OHAN DIATH SHIIBHA
NOIIBHA BHAHAN**

- Draw the portal clockwise and leave the south side of the portal open.

➤ Place the **CEDAR** incense in the center of the circle and a **WHITE** or **PURPLE** candle inside the outer design at the north end. Then light them up.
➤ Finish the drawing by closing the portal

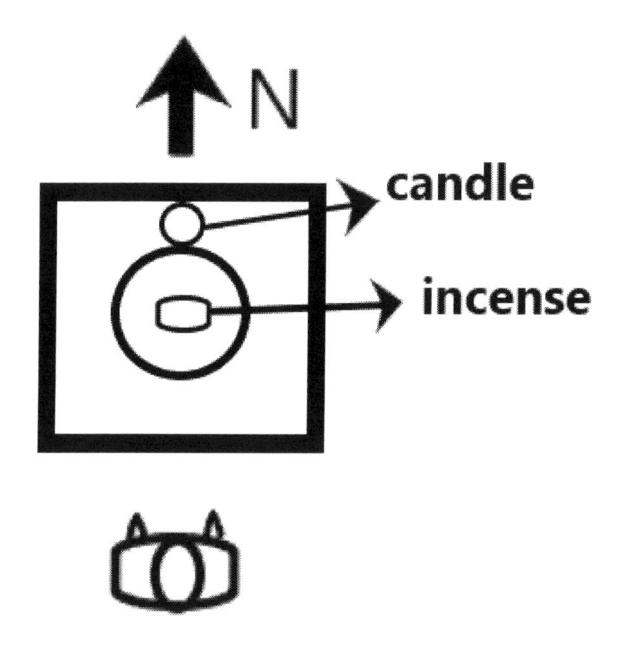

- Turn off the light.
- Standing with your hands at your sides, recite the invitation:

"NAMAHA HUASH SHIAN SHANABHI KOAN"

- Wait a few seconds in silence.
- Draw the key in the air in front of the portal.

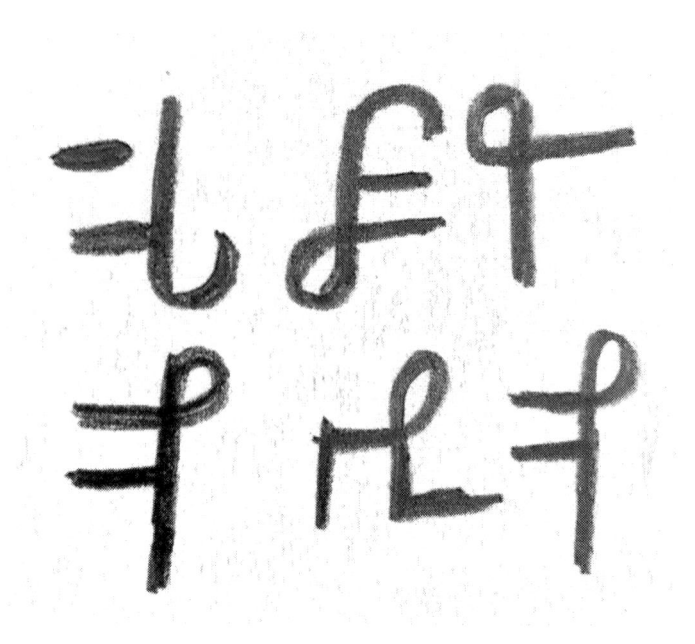

- ➤ Wait a few seconds.
- ➤ Now recite the evocation 3 times:

"NAMAHA VANOILTH NARA SHOTHSH TIBHARA"

- ➤ Wait a few minutes and if you do not feel the presence of Vanoilth repeat the above evocation 3 more times.
- ➤ Wait a few minutes.
- ➤ If Vanoilth has not yet manifested, recite the second evocation 3 times.

"SHOTHSH RIUNA VANOILTH KOAN NAMAHA"

- At the end of the third recitation it will be there, whether you feel it or not.
- Throw the piece of paper with your order into the portal. You can write the request on paper before or at that time of the ritual, in the presence of Vanoilth.
- Mentalize the order for a minimum of 5 minutes, imagine your order being fulfilled, feel the emotion.
- After you have mentalized, say:

"I am grateful to Vanoilth for having heard my call and I am grateful for the request made."

- End the ritual
- Trace the double pentagram in the air and at the same time vibrate the words of power:

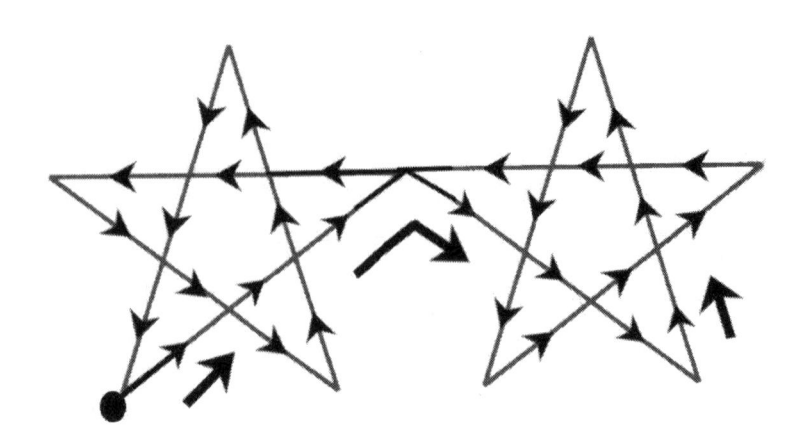

NAHAWAI NOHONAI NAMAHA NAMENIHI KOAN BHALIHI

- ➢ Exit the room and let the candle and incense burn to the end.
- ➢ Come back 24 hours later to clean up.
- ➢ Go back to your normal routine and wait for the results of the ritual without anxiety or doubt.

Meltrafon

SPECIALTIES

- ➢ Fast learning.
- ➢ Quick thinking.
- ➢ Victory in all discussions.
- ➢ Cause leprosy in an enemy.
- ➢ Get rich using reasoning.
- ➢ To cause violent death to an enemy.
- ➢ Leading an enemy to suicide.

GOETIA

- ➢ Corresponds to Andrealphus.

RITUAL

- ➢ To the north.
- ➢ Trace the double pentagram in the air and at the same time vibrate the words of power:

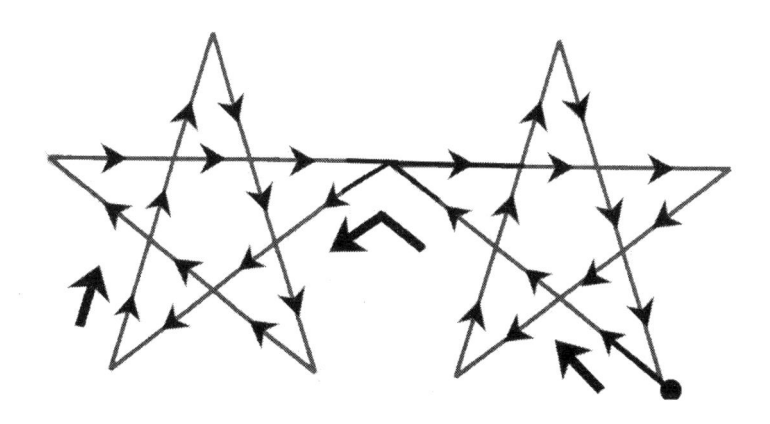

NAHAWAH KABIH OHAN DIATH SHIIBHA NOIIBHA BHAHAN

➢ Draw the portal clockwise and leave the south side of the portal open.

- ➢ Place the **FLOWER** incense in the center of the circle and a **WHITE** candle inside the outer design at the north end. Then light them up.
- ➢ Finish the drawing by closing the portal.

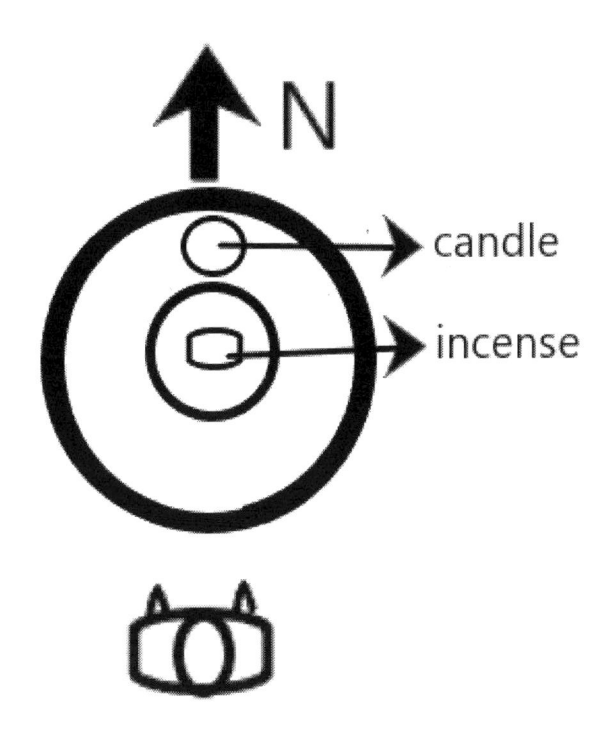

- ➢ Turn off the light.
- ➢ Standing with your hands at your sides, recite the invitation:

"THANIBHA HUANI SHIAN BHIASH HUABHI"

- ➢ Wait a few seconds in silence.

- ➢ Draw the key in the air in front of the portal.

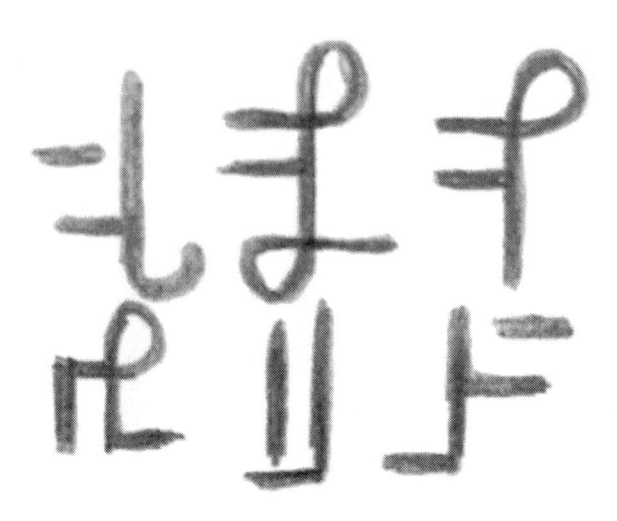

- ➢ Wait a few seconds.
- ➢ Now recite the evocation 3 times:

"MELTRAFON BHIAKSI KOAN HUABHI NANABHI"

- ➢ Wait a few minutes and if you do not feel the presence of Meltrafon repeat the above evocation 3 more times.
- ➢ Wait a few minutes.

- If Meltrafon has not yet manifested, recite the second evocation 3 times.

"BHIAKSI KOAN HUABHI MELTRAFON TIBHARA"

- At the end of the third recitation it will be there, whether you feel it or not.
- Throw the piece of paper with your order into the portal. You can write the request on paper before or at that moment of the ritual, in the presence of Meltrafon.
- Mentalize the order for a minimum of 5 minutes, imagine your order being fulfilled, feel the emotion.
- After you have mentalized, say:

"I thank Meltrafon for having heard my call and thank you for the request."

- End the ritual.
- Trace the double pentagram in the air and at the same time vibrate the words of power:

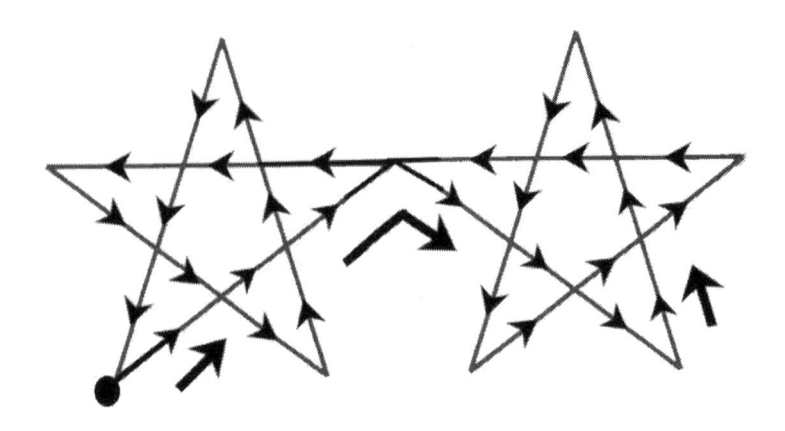

NAHAWAI NOHONAI NAMAHA NAMENIHI KOAN BHALIHI

- Exit the room and let the candle and incense burn to the end.
- Come back 24 hours later to clean up.
- Go back to your normal routine and wait for the results of the ritual without anxiety or doubt.

Noabhind

SPECIALTIES

- ➢ Get stable source of income.
- ➢ Make groups of people admire you.
- ➢ Get customers to trade.

- ➢ Get allies.
- ➢ Make money by investing.
- ➢ Driving enemy to suicide by hanging.
- ➢ Making enemy self-sabotage.

GOETIA

- ➢ It corresponds to Camio.

RITUAL

- ➢ To the north.
- ➢ Trace the double pentagram in the air and at the same time vibrate the words of power:

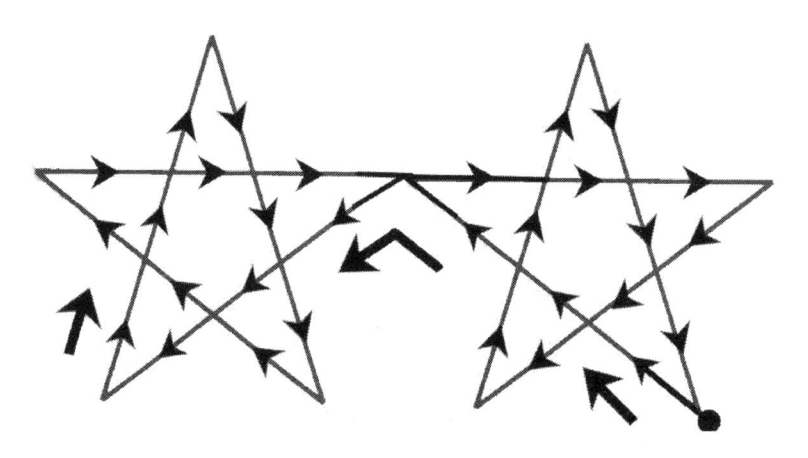

NAHAWAH KABIH OHAN DIATH SHIIBHA NOIIBHA BHAHAN

> Draw the portal clockwise and leave the south side of the portal open.

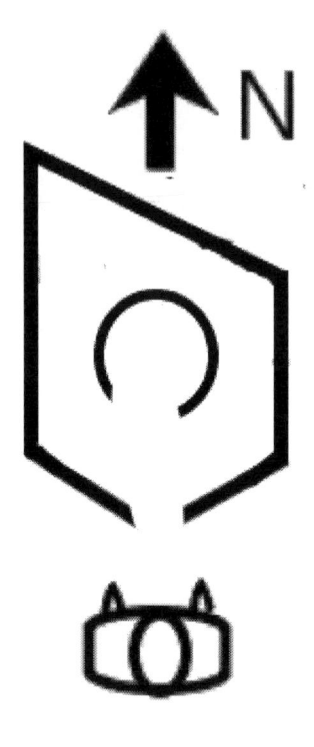

- Place the **MYRRH** or **SAGE** incense in the center of the circle and a **GOLD** or **ORANGE** candle inside the outer design at the north end. Then light them.
- Finish the drawing by closing the portal.

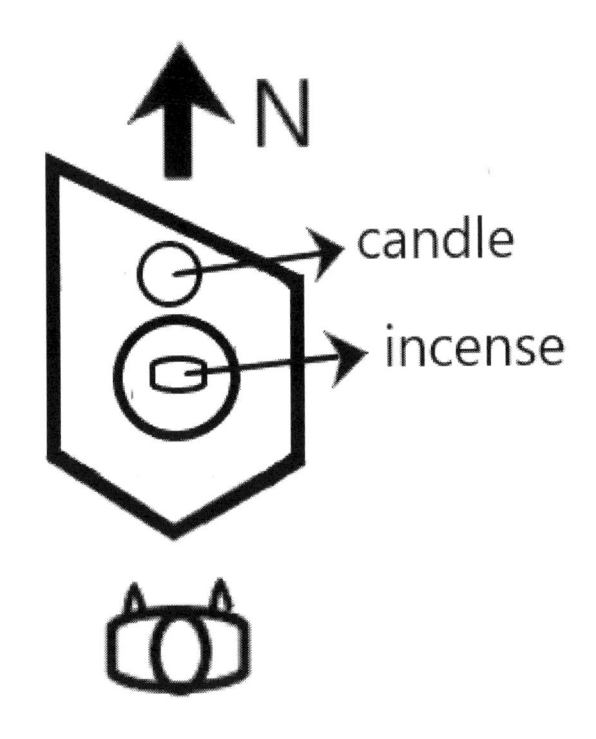

- Turn off the light.

- Standing with your hands close to your body, recite the invitation:

"KATHIBHA THANIBHA NOAN NANATHE HASHIBHU"

- Wait a few seconds in silence.

- Draw the key in the air in front of the portal.

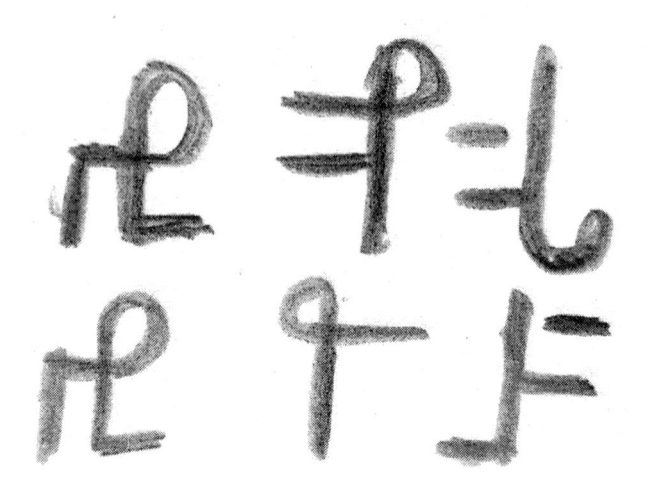

- Wait a few seconds.

- Now recite the evocation 3 times:

"KARIAH KARANA NOABHIND RIUH KABHAD AURE PAMDARAH"

- Wait a few minutes and if you don't feel Noabhind's presence repeat the above evocation 3 more times.
- Wait a few minutes.

- If Noabhind has not yet manifested, recite the second evocation 3 times.

"NOA NOABHIND DEREK KOAN NAGARA SHIIBHA"

- At the end of the third recitation it will be there, whether you feel it or not.
- Throw the piece of paper with your order inside the portal. You can write the request on paper before or at this time of the ritual, in Noabhind's presence.
- Mind the request for at least 5 minutes, imagine your request being carried out, feel the emotion.
- After having mentalized, say:

"I thank Noabhind for having heard my call and I thank him for his request."

- End the ritual.
- Trace the double pentagram in the air and at the same time vibrate the words of power:

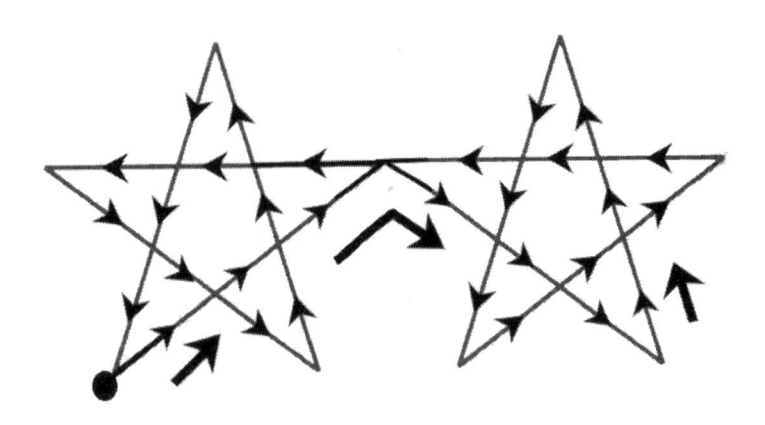

NAHAWAI NOHONAI NAMAHA NAMENIHI KOAN BHALIHI

- Leave the room and let the candle and incense burn to the end.
- Come back 24 hours later to clean everything up.
- Get back to your normal routine and wait for the results of the ritual without anxiety or doubt.

Bhoran

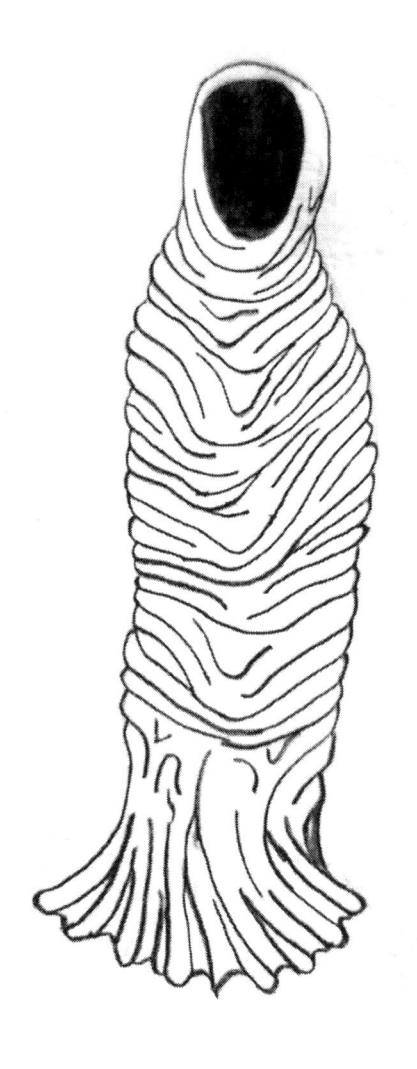

SPECIALTIES

- Obtain mineral riches.
- Find gold easily.
- Get cash flow.
- Make a financial profit in any business.
- Get lucky in games of chance.
- Drive the enemy to misery.

GOETIA

- It corresponds to Bathin.

RITUAL

- To the north.
- Trace the double pentagram in the air and at the same time vibrate the words of power:

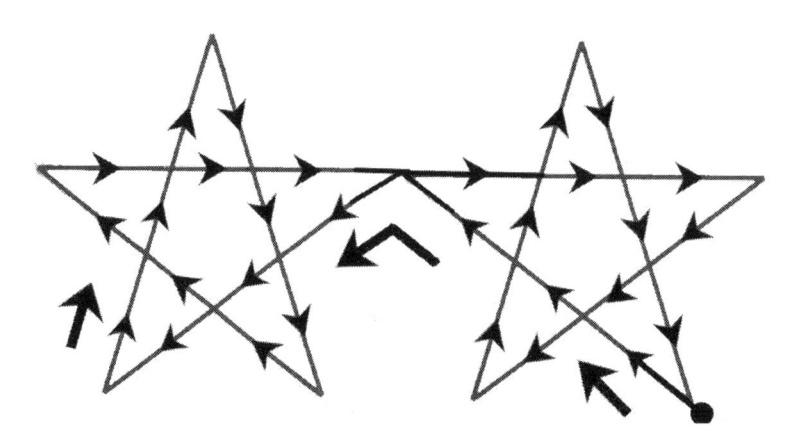

NAHAWAH KABIH OHAN DIATH SHIIBHA NOIIBHA BHAHAN

> Draw the portal clockwise and leave the south side of the portal open.

- Place **CEDAR** incense in the center of the circle and a **BLUE** or **BLACK** candle inside the design at the north end. Then light them.
- Finish the drawing by closing the portal.

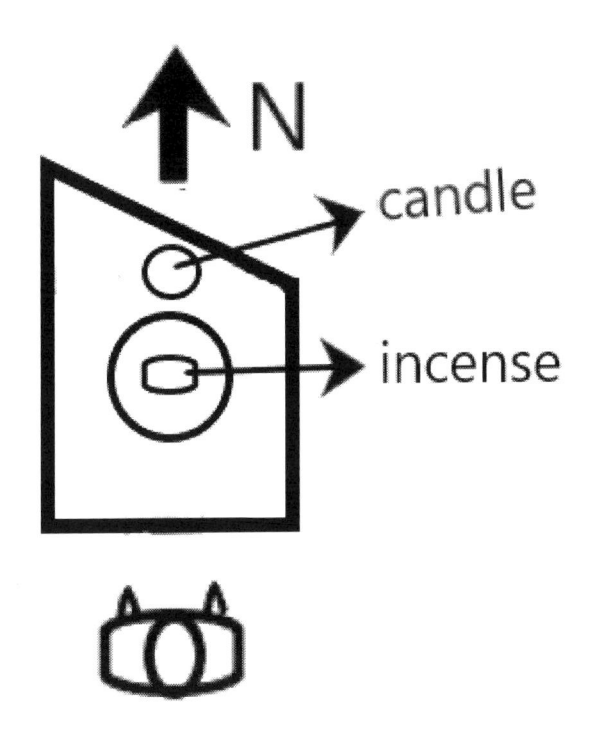

- Turn off the light.

- Standing with your hands close to your body, recite the invitation:

"KANIBHA THARON THANIBHA HASHIBHU BANIBHU"

- ➢ Wait a few seconds in silence.

- ➢ Draw the key in the air in front of the portal.

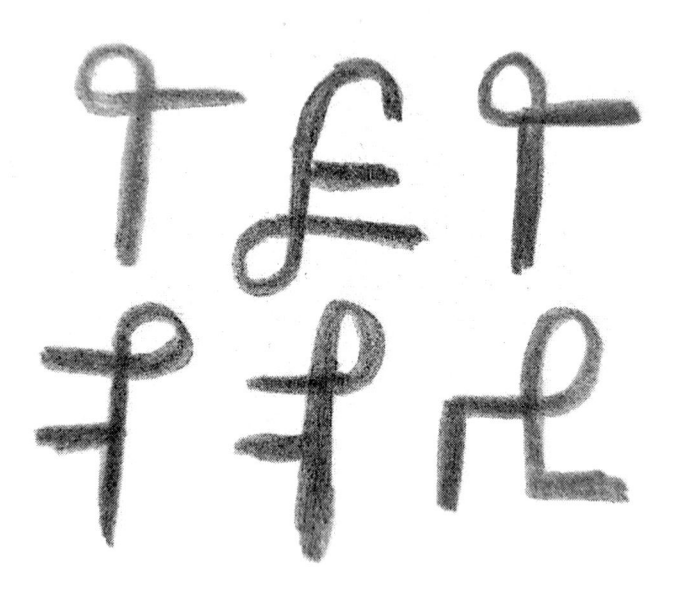

- ➢ Wait a few seconds.

- ➢ Now recite the evocation 3 times:

"KARANA MASHIBHA PURANA BHORAN KASHID SHORANA PAMDARAH"

- ➢ Wait a few minutes and if you don't feel Bhoran's presence repeat the above evocation 3 more times.
- ➢ Wait a few minutes.

- ➢ If Bhoran has not yet manifested, recite the second evocation 3 times.

"BHORAN RIUNA KOAN NAGARA SHIBOM"

- ➢ At the end of the third recitation it will be there, whether you feel it or not.
- ➢ Throw the piece of paper with your order inside the portal. You can write the request on paper before or at this time of the ritual, in the presence of Bhoran.
- ➢ Mind the request for at least 5 minutes, imagine your request being carried out, feel the emotion.
- ➢ After having mentalized, say:

"I am grateful to Bhoran for having heard my call and I am grateful for the request made."

- End the ritual.
- Trace the double pentagram in the air and at the same time vibrate the words of power:

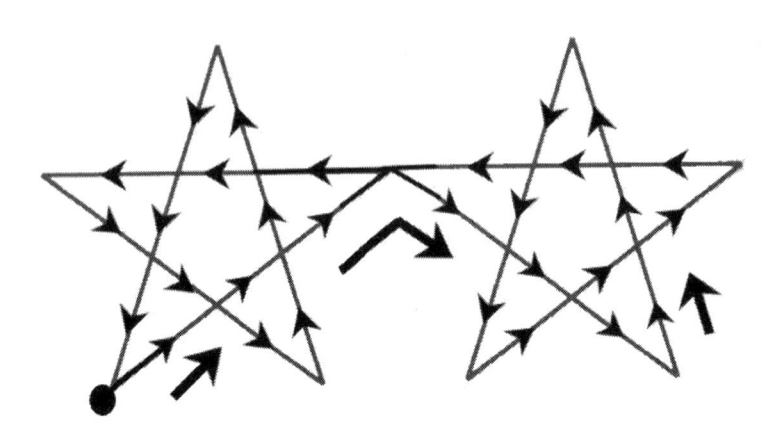

NAHAWAI NOHONAI NAMAHA NAMENIHI KOAN BHALIHI

- Leave the room and let the candle and incense burn to the end.
- Come back 24 hours later to clean everything up.
- Get back to your normal routine and wait for the results of the ritual without anxiety or doubt.

Nathandha

SPECIALTIES

- Achieve meaning in life.
- Bring self-confidence.
- Get cash flow.
- Succeed in all areas.
- Get political power.
- Humiliate enemy.

GOETIA

- Corresponds to Oriax.

RITUAL

- To the north.
- Trace the double pentagram in the air and at the same time vibrate the words of power:

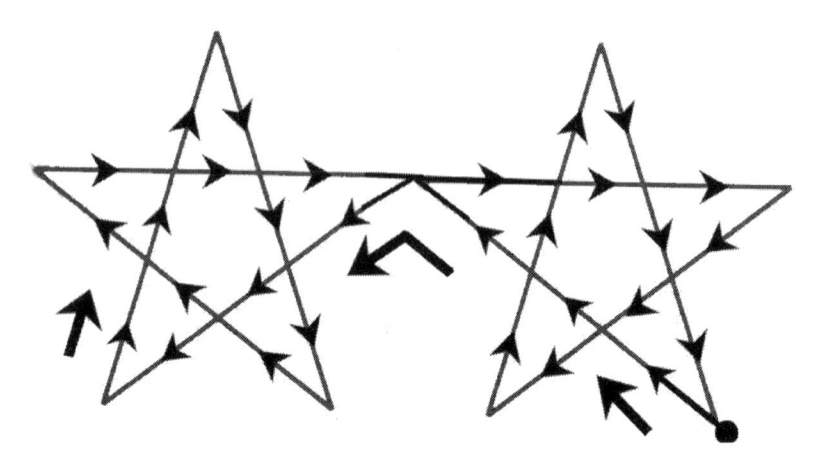

NAHAWAH KABIH OHAN DIATH SHIIBHA NOIIBHA BHAHAN

➢ Draw the portal clockwise and leave the south side of the portal open.

➢ Place **VANILLA** incense in the center of the circle and a **WHITE** or **BROWN** candle inside the design at the north end. Then light them.

➢ Finish the drawing by closing the portal.

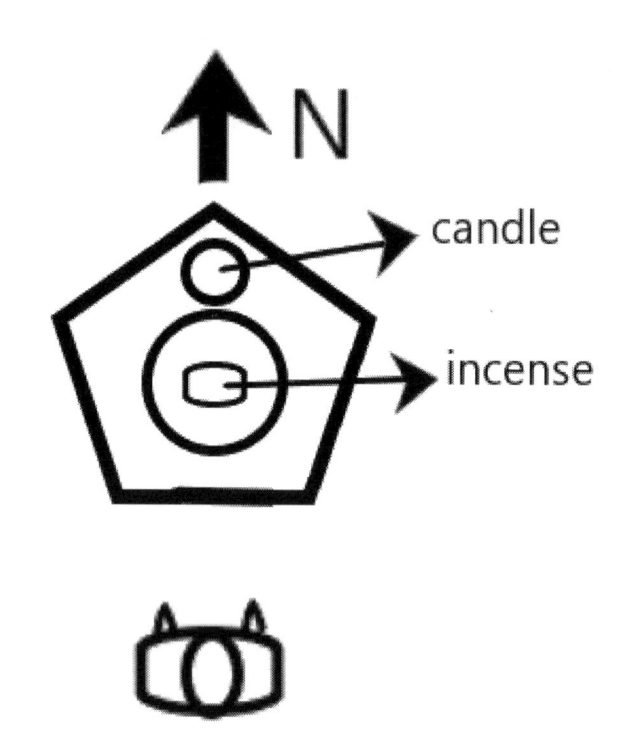

    ⬆ N

    → candle

    → incense

➢ Turn off the light.

➢ Standing with your hands close to your body, recite the invitation:

"KANIBHA THATHABHA HUABHI NANIBHI HASHIBHU"

- Wait a few seconds in silence.

- Draw the key in the air in front of the portal.

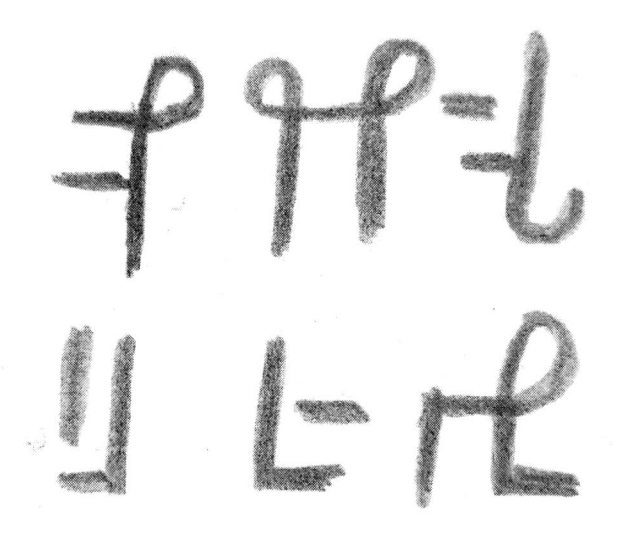

- Wait a few seconds.

- Now recite the evocation 3 times:

"KARANA NATHANDHA SHORANA PAMDARAH KOAN"

- Wait a few minutes and if you don't feel Nathandha's presence repeat the above evocation 3 more times.
- Wait a few minutes.

- If Nathandha has not yet manifested, recite the second evocation 3 times.

"NATHANDHA KARANA KOAN NAGARA NAMAHA"

- At the end of the third recitation it will be there, whether you feel it or not.
- Throw the piece of paper with your order inside the portal. You can write the request on paper before or at this time of the ritual, in Nathandha's presence.
- Mind the request for at least 5 minutes, imagine your request being carried out, feel the emotion.
- After having mentalized, say:

"I am grateful to Nathandha for having heard my call and I am grateful for the request made."

- ➢ End the ritual.
- ➢ Trace the double pentagram in the air and at the same time vibrate the words of power:

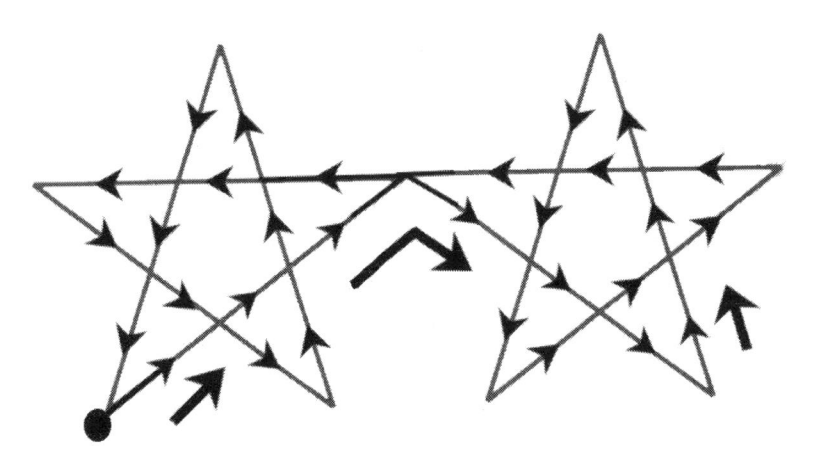

NAHAWAI NOHONAI NAMAHA NAMENIHI KOAN BHALIHI

- ➢ Leave the room and let the candle and incense burn to the end.
- ➢ Come back 24 hours later to clean everything up.

- Get back to your normal routine and wait for the results of the ritual without anxiety or doubt.

Hanthal

SPECIALTIES

- Solve difficult problems.
- Bring tranquility.
- Increase financial profits.
- Achieve good placement in competitions.
- Make someone loyal to you.
- Cause painful death to enemy.

GOETIA

- Corresponds to Vapula.

RITUAL

- To the north.
- Trace the double pentagram in the air and at the same time vibrate the words of power:

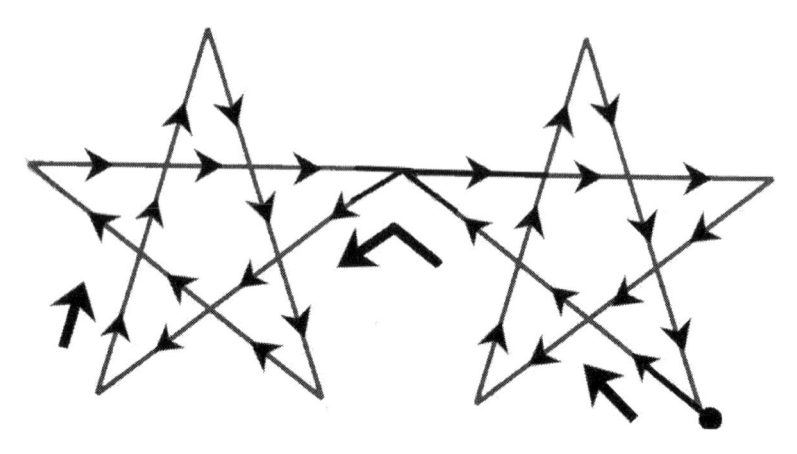

NAHAWAH KABIH OHAN DIATH SHIIBHA NOIIBHA BHAHAN

➢ Draw the portal clockwise and leave the south side of the portal open.

➢ Place **PATCHOULI** incense in the center of the circle and a **WHITE** or **BLUE** candle inside the design at the north end. Then light them.

➢ Finish the drawing by closing the portal.

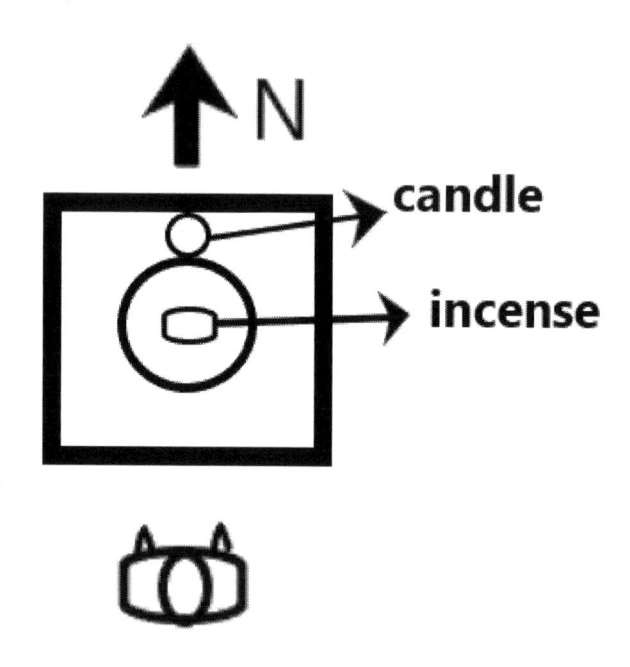

candle

incense

➢ Turn off the light.

➢ Standing with your hands close to your body, recite the invitation:

"KABHASH THANIBHA HUSHIBHI NANIBHA HASHIBHU"

- ➢ Wait a few seconds in silence.

- ➢ Draw the key in the air in front of the portal.

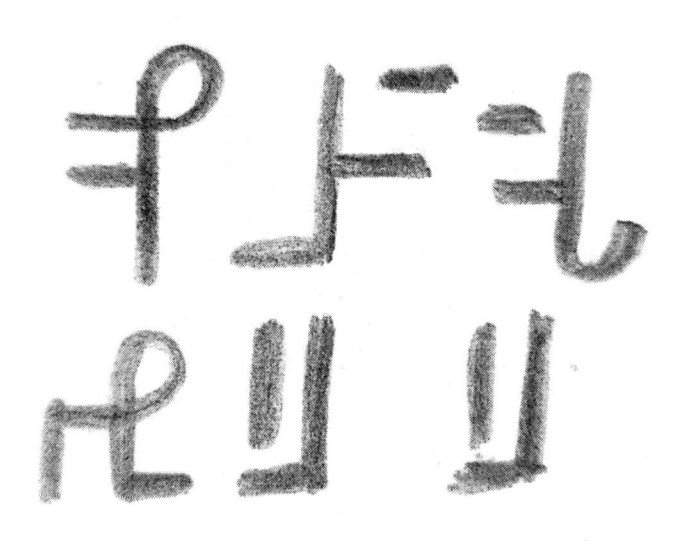

- ➢ Wait a few seconds.

- ➢ Now recite the evocation 3 times:

"HANTHAL KARANA HASHIBHU KARASHI SHORANA PARARAH"

- Wait a few minutes and if you don't feel Hanthal's presence repeat the above evocation 3 more times.
- Wait a few minutes.

- If Hanthal has not yet manifested, recite the second evocation 3 times.

"HANTHAL SHORANA RIUNA SHIRIBHA"

- At the end of the third recitation it will be there, whether you feel it or not.
- Throw the piece of paper with your order inside the portal. You can write the request on paper before or at this time of the ritual, in Hanthal's presence.
- Mind the request for at least 5 minutes, imagine your request being carried out, feel the emotion.
- After having mentalized, say:

"I thank Hanthal for having listened to my call and I thank him for his request."

- End the ritual.
- Trace the double pentagram in the air and at the same time vibrate the words of power:

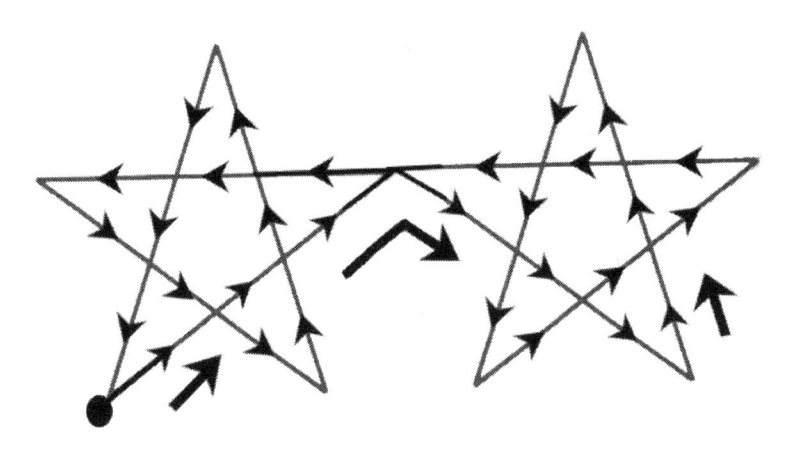

NAHAWAI NOHONAI NAMAHA NAMENIHI KOAN BHALIHI

- Leave the room and let the candle and incense burn to the end.
- Come back 24 hours later to clean everything up.
- Get back to your normal routine and wait for the results of the ritual without anxiety or doubt.

Shisthenoalgho

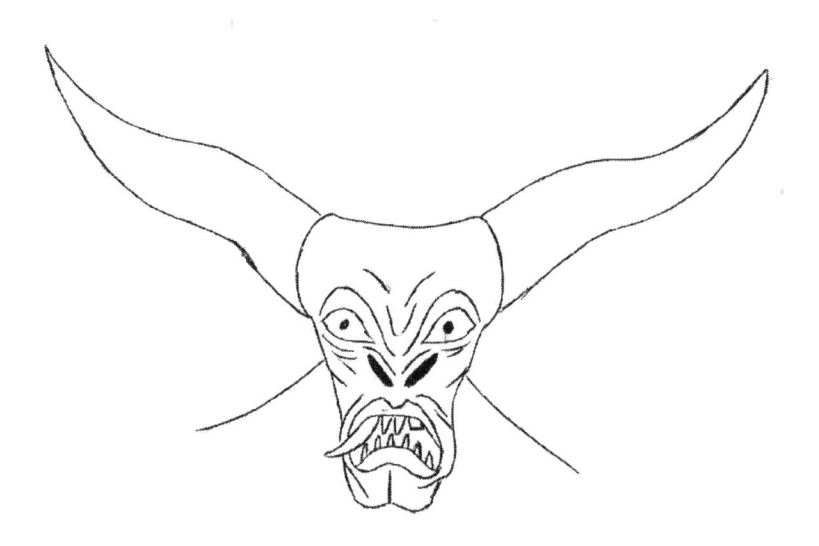

SPECIALTIES

- Receive a large cash donation
- Cause all sorts of trouble to an enemy.
- To cause fear and oppress those who are arrogant.
- Find hidden riches.

GOETIA

- Corresponds to Vepar.

RITUAL

- To the north.
- Trace the double pentagram in the air and at the same time vibrate the words of power:

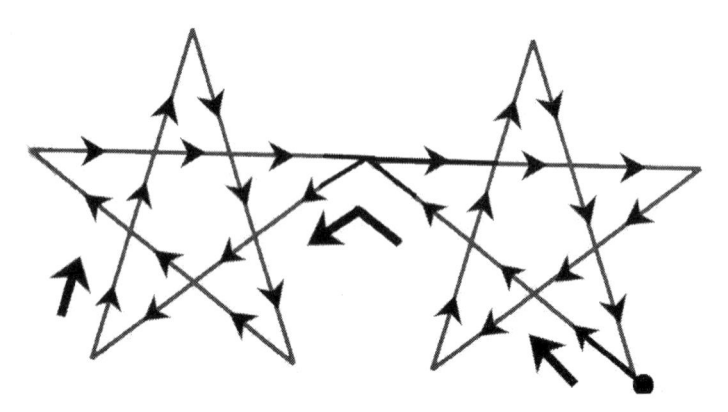

NAHAWAH KABIH OHAN DIATH SHIIBHA NOIIBHA BHAHAN

- Draw the portal clockwise and leave the south side of the portal open.

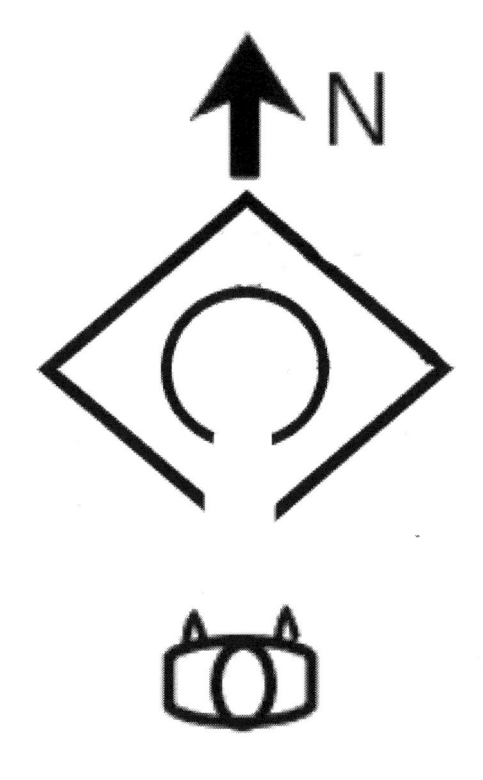

- Place the **MYRRH** incense in the center of the circle and a **BLACK** candle inside the square at the north end. Then light them.
- Finish the drawing by closing the portal.

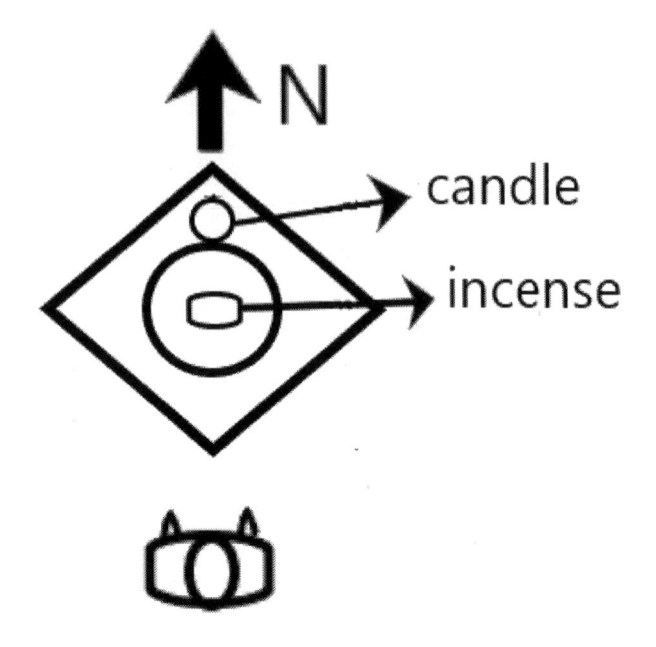

➤ Turn off the light.

➤ Pierce your finger and place 1 drop of blood inside the inner circle
➤ wait a few seconds

214

- Standing with your hands close to your body, recite the invitation:

"KANIBHA THANIBHA HUABHI NANABHI HASHIBHU BANIBHU"

- Wait a few seconds in silence.

- Draw the key in the air in front of the portal.

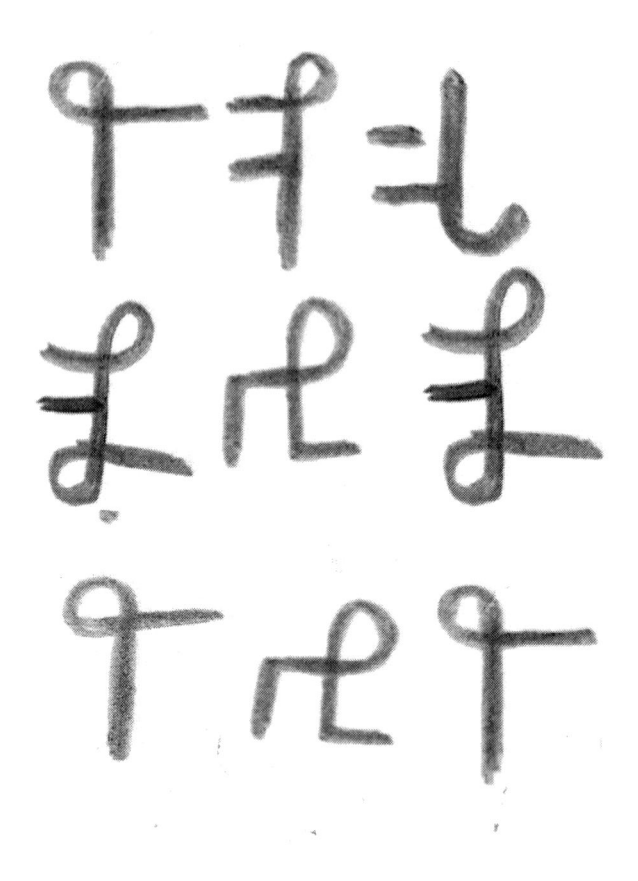

- Wait a few seconds.

- Now recite the evocation 3 times:

"SHISTHENOALGHO NOIIBHA BHAHAN KARANA RIUNA SHORANA"

- Wait a few minutes and if you don't feel Shisthenoalgho's presence repeat the above evocation 3 more times.
- Wait a few minutes.

- If Shisthenoalgho has not yet manifested, recite the second evocation 3 times.

"NOIIBHA SHISTHENOALGHO BHAHAN NAGARA SHIBOM KARANA"

- At the end of the third recitation it will be there, whether you feel it or not.
- Throw the piece of paper with your order inside the portal. You can write the request on paper before or at this time of the ritual, in the presence of Shisthenoalgho.
- Envision the request for at least 5 minutes, imagine your request taking place, feel the emotion.
- After having mentalized, say:

"I am grateful to Shisthenoalgho for having heard my call and I am grateful for the request made."

- End the ritual.
- Trace the double pentagram in the air and at the same time vibrate the words of power:

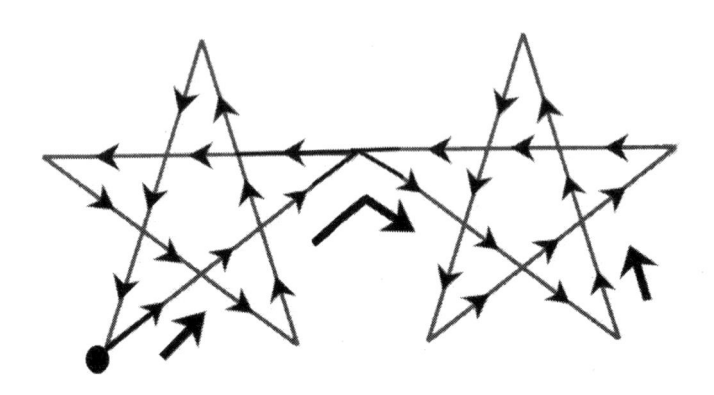

NAHAWAI NOHONAI NAMAHA NAMENIHI KOAN BHALIHI

- Leave the room and let the candle and incense burn to the end.
- Come back 24 hours later to clean everything up.
- Get back to your normal routine and wait for the results of the ritual without anxiety or doubt.

Malentha

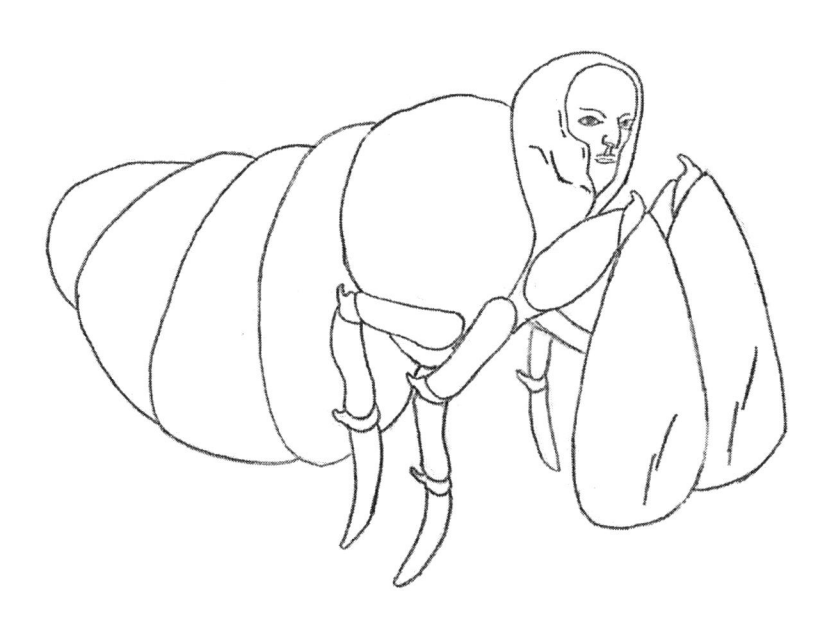

SPECIALTIES

- Achieve a luxurious life.
- Bring material comfort.
- Get cash flow.
- Getting money from food and agriculture.
- Have a good reputation.
- Protect you from bad people.

GOETIA

- Corresponds to Lerage.

RITUAL

- To the north.
- Trace the double pentagram in the air and at the same time vibrate the words of power:

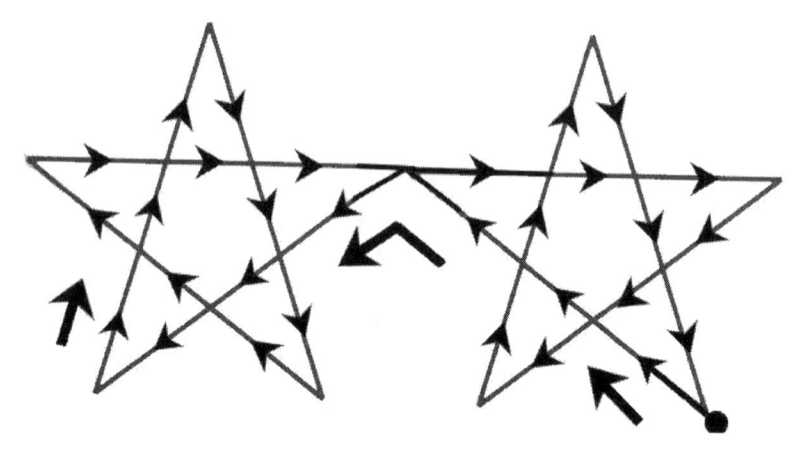

NAHAWAH KABIH OHAN DIATH SHIIBHA NOIIBHA BHAHAN

- Draw the portal clockwise and leave the south side of the portal open.

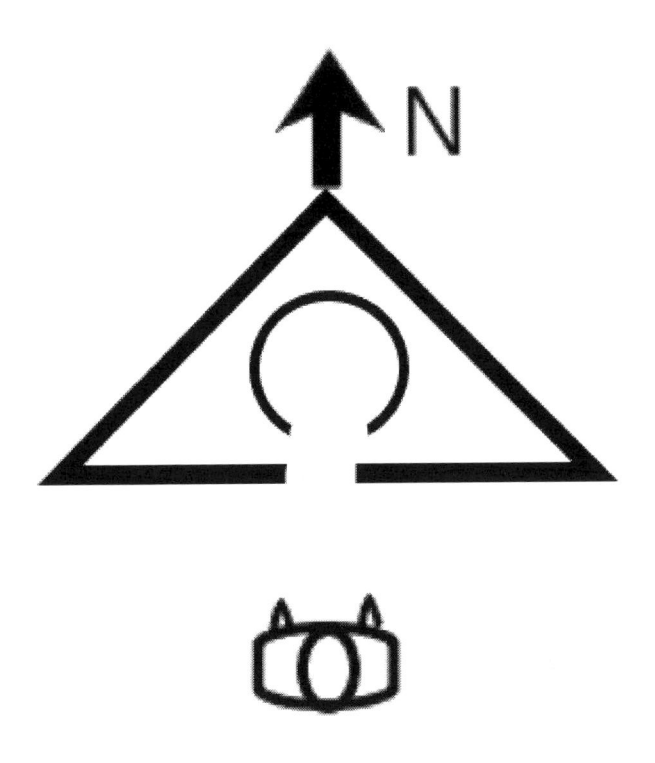

- Place **ROSEMARY** or **JASMINE** incense in the center of the circle and a **BLACK** or **YELLOW** candle inside the design at the north end. Then light them.
- Finish the drawing by closing the portal.

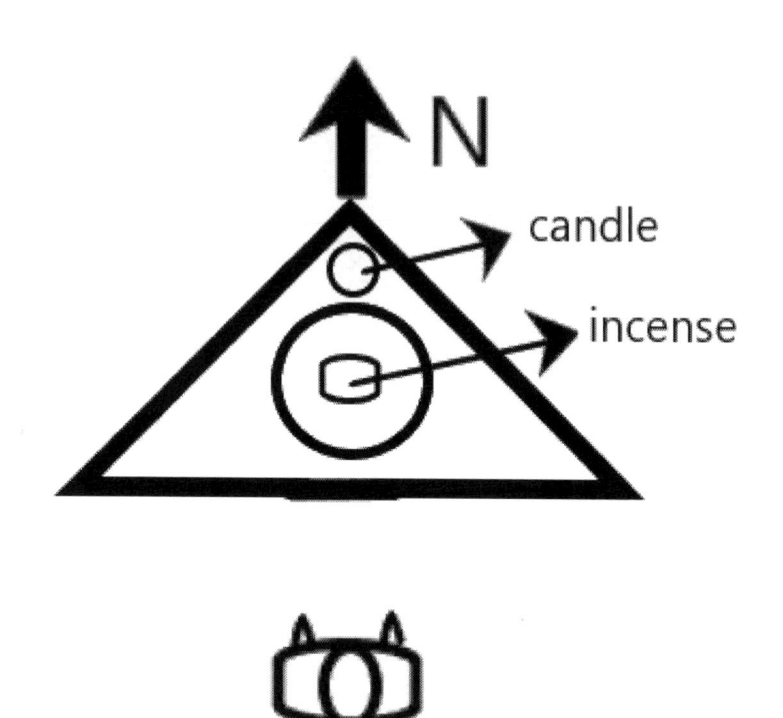

- Turn off the light.

- Standing with your hands close to your body, recite the invitation:

"KANIBHA NANIBHA HASHIBHI NANABHI HASHIBHU BANIBHU"

- ➢ Wait a few seconds in silence.

- ➢ Draw the key in the air in front of the portal.

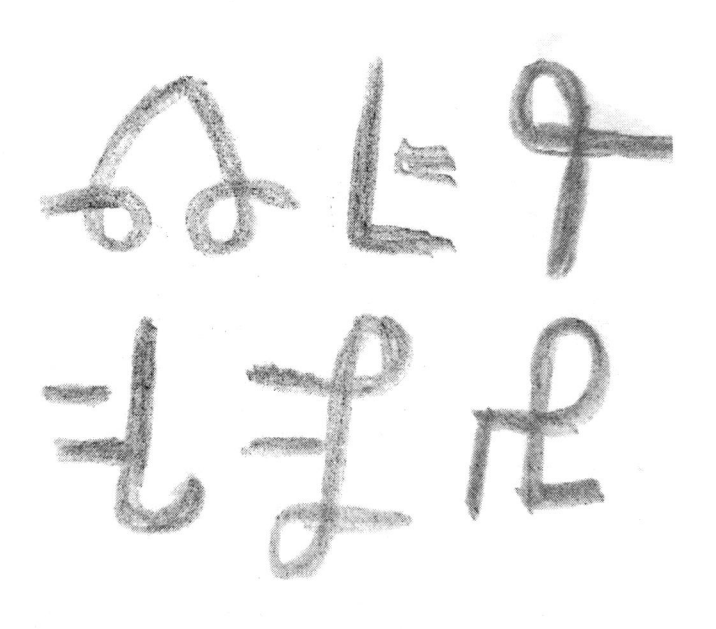

- ➢ Wait a few seconds.

- ➢ Now recite the evocation 3 times:

"MALENTHA NAMASH PORAN RIASH KASHID SHORABHA"

- Wait a few minutes and if you don't feel Malentha's presence repeat the above evocation 3 more times.
- Wait a few minutes.

- If Malentha has not yet manifested, recite the second evocation 3 times.

"KOAN MALENTHA RIUNA NAGARA SHIRANH"

- At the end of the third recitation it will be there, whether you feel it or not.
- Throw the piece of paper with your order inside the portal. You can write the request on paper before or at this time of the ritual, in Malentha's presence.
- Mind the request for at least 5 minutes, imagine your request being carried out, feel the emotion.
- After having mentalized, say:

"I am grateful to Malentha for having heard my call and I am grateful for her request."

- End the ritual.
- Trace the double pentagram in the air and at the same time vibrate the words of power:

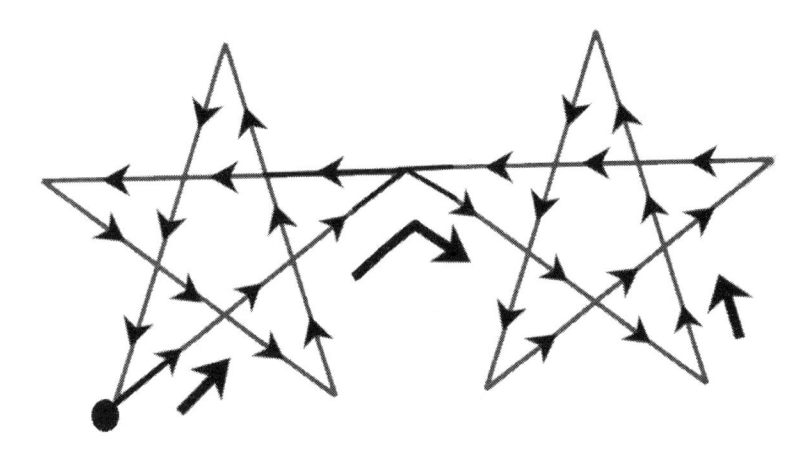

NAHAWAI NOHONAI NAMAHA NAMENIHI KOAN BHALIHI

- Leave the room and let the candle and incense burn to the end.
- Come back 24 hours later to clean everything up.

- Get back to your normal routine and wait for the results of the ritual without anxiety or doubt.

Khoril

SPECIALTIES

- Protection against any type of attack.
- Protection of chosen people
- Enable you to counter attack efficiently.
- Cause leprosy in a chosen person.
- Achieve loyal allies.
- Get people to work for you.

GOETIA

- It corresponds to Sabnock.

RITUAL

- To the north.
- Trace the double pentagram in the air and at the same time vibrate the words of power:

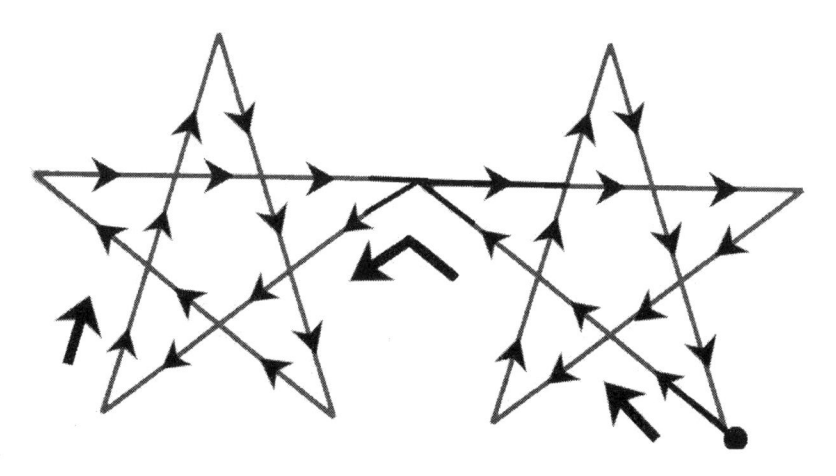

NAHAWAH KABIH OHAN DIATH SHIIBHA NOIIBHA BHAHAN

- Draw the portal clockwise and leave the south side of the portal open.

- Place **ROSE** or **LAVENDER** incense in the center of the circle and a **WHITE** candle inside the design at the north end. Then light them.
- Finish the drawing by closing the portal.

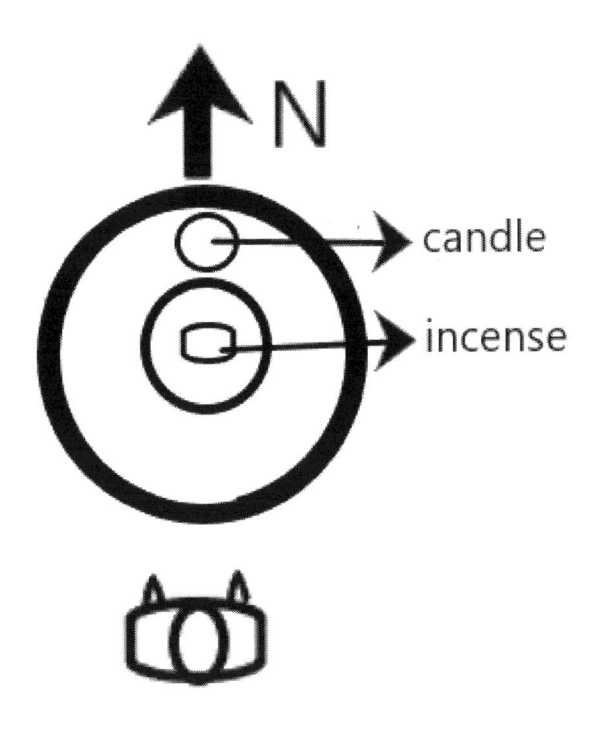

➢ Turn off the light.

➢ Standing with your hands close to your body, recite the invitation:

"THANIBHA NAMAH HUABHI NANIBHA BANIBHAH"

➢ Wait a few seconds in silence.

➢ Draw the key in the air in front of the portal.

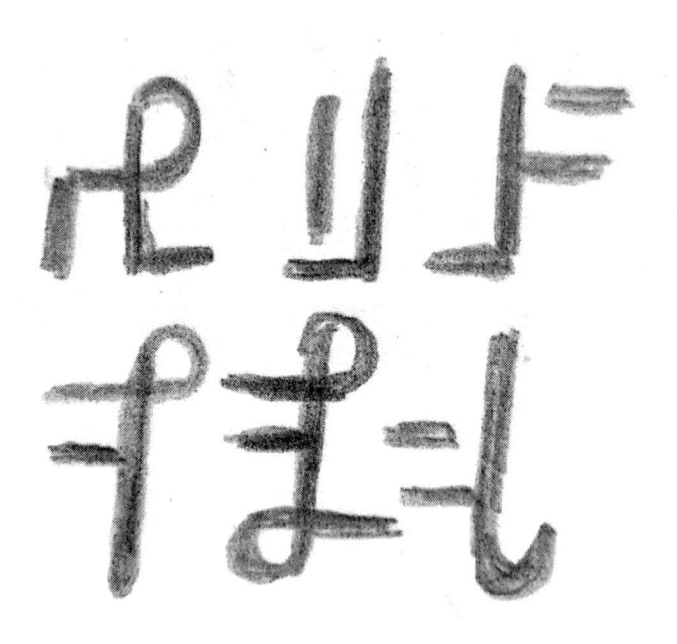

➢ Wait a few seconds.

➢ Now recite the evocation 3 times:

"KHORIL KIV PARANA RIUNA PAMDARAH HUABHI"

- Wait a few minutes and if you don't feel Khoril's presence repeat the above evocation 3 more times.
- Wait a few minutes.

- If Khoril has not yet manifested, recite the second evocation 3 times.

"KHORIL NANABHI KOAN SHIBOM BHAHAN"

- At the end of the third recitation it will be there, whether you feel it or not.
- Throw the piece of paper with your order inside the portal. You can write the request on paper before or at this time of the ritual, in Khoril's presence.
- Mind the request for at least 5 minutes, imagine your request being carried out, feel the emotion.
- After having mentalized, say:

"I thank Khoril for having heard my call and I thank him for the request made."

- ➤ End the ritual.
- ➤ Trace the double pentagram in the air and at the same time vibrate the words of power:

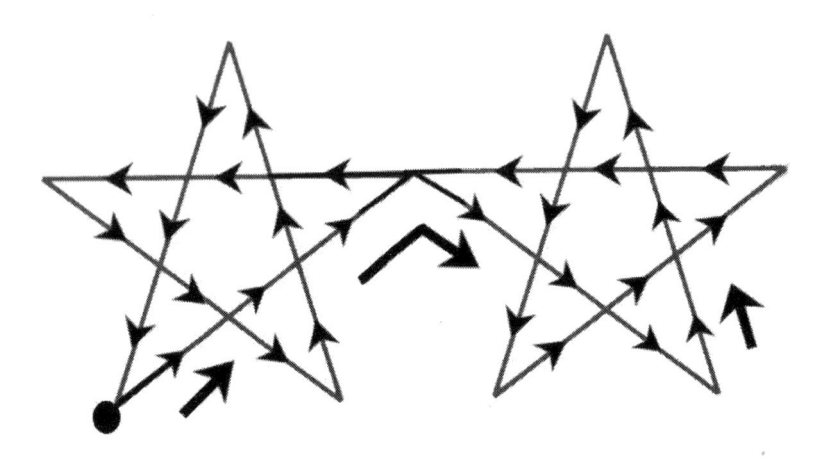

NAHAWAI NOHONAI NAMAHA NAMENIHI KOAN BHALIHI

- ➤ Leave the room and let the candle and incense burn to the end.
- ➤ Come back 24 hours later to clean everything up.
- ➤ Get back to your normal routine and wait for the results of the ritual without anxiety or doubt.

Patheo

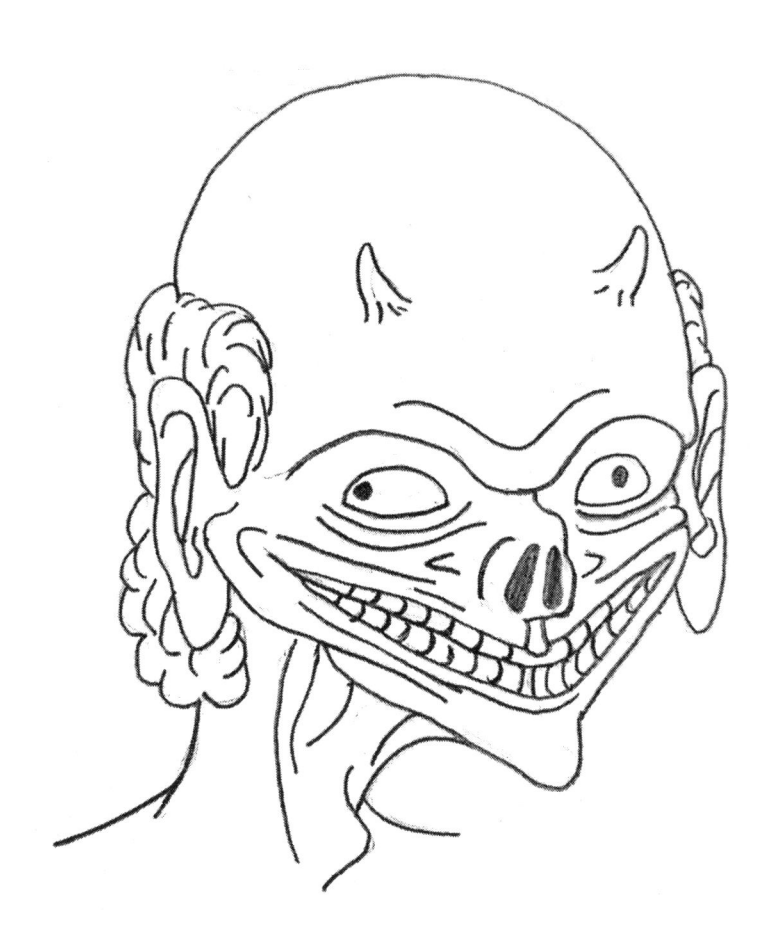

SPECIALTIES

- Generates sexual attraction in the chosen person.
- Generates hatred between two people or group of people.
- Cause conflicts in environments chosen by you.
- Make people believe something that isn't true.
- Make your enemy obey your orders.
- Bring advantages and benefits for you.

GOETIA

- Corresponds to Ronove.

RITUAL

- To the north.
- Trace the double pentagram in the air and at the same time vibrate the words of power:

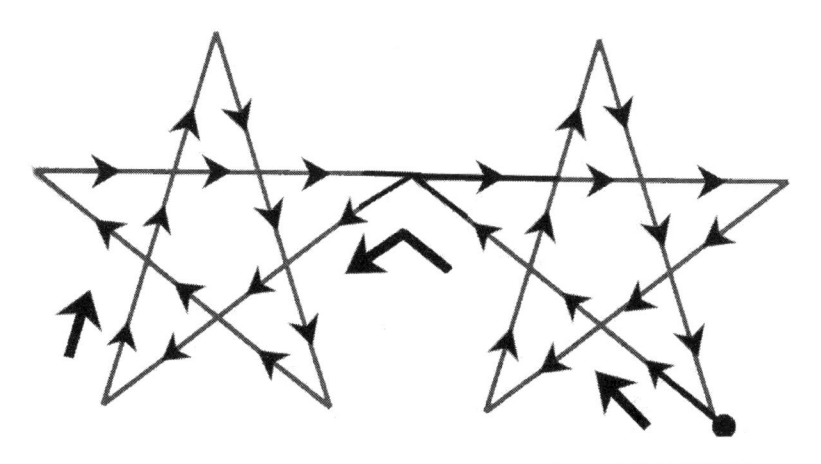

NAHAWAH KABIH OHAN DIATH SHIIBHA NOIIBHA BHAHAN

- Draw the portal clockwise and leave the south side of the portal open.

- Place the **LEMON** incense in the center of the circle and a **WHITE** or **GREEN** candle inside the design at the north end. Then light them.
- Finish the drawing by closing the portal.

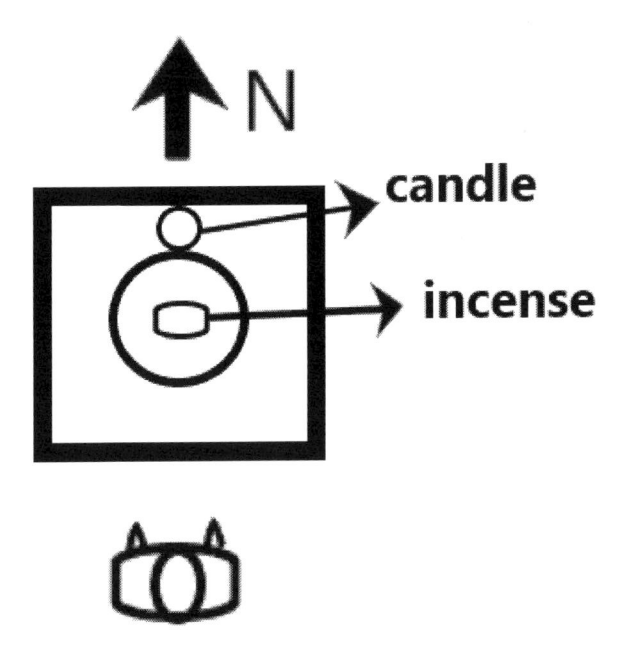

- Turn off the light.

- Standing with your hands close to your body, recite the invitation:

"NANABHI HASHIBHU BANIBHU KANIBHA THANIBHA HUABHI"

- Wait a few seconds in silence.

➢ Draw the key in the air in front of the portal.

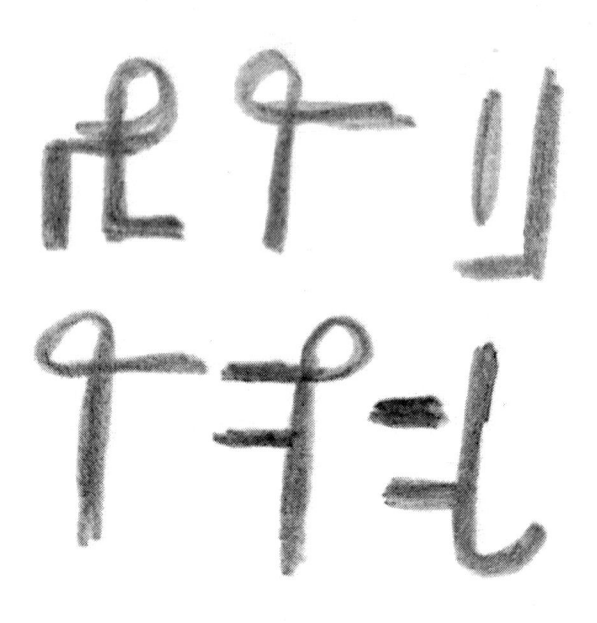

➢ Wait a few seconds.

➢ Now recite the evocation 3 times:

"HUABHI PATHEO KARANA NANABHI SHORANA HUABHI"

- Wait a few minutes and if you don't feel Patheo's presence repeat the above evocation 3 more times.
- Wait a few minutes.

- If Patheo has not yet manifested, recite the second evocation 3 times.

"PATHEO RIUNA KARANA NANABHI HASHIBHU"

- At the end of the third recitation it will be there, whether you feel it or not.
- Throw the piece of paper with your order inside the portal. You can write the request on paper before or at this time of the ritual, in the presence of Patheo.
- Mind the request for at least 5 minutes, imagine your request being carried out, feel the emotion.
- After having mentalized, say:

"I am grateful to Patheo for having heard my call and I am grateful for the request made."

- End the ritual.
- Trace the double pentagram in the air and at the same time vibrate the words of power:

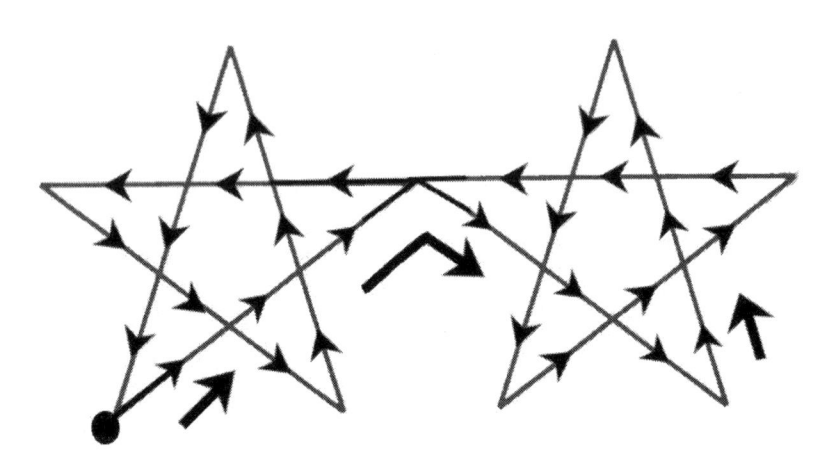

NAHAWAI NOHONAI NAMAHA NAMENIHI KOAN BHALIHI

- Leave the room and let the candle and incense burn to the end.
- Come back 24 hours later to clean everything up.
- Get back to your normal routine and wait for the results of the ritual without anxiety or doubt.

Chrisnonbh

SPECIALTIES

- Bring prosperity.
- Make an enemy not distrust attack and put no resistance.
- Cause mental confusion.
- Make you profit from enemy damage
- Bring success in the area of buying and selling real estate

GOETIA

- It corresponds to Shax.

RITUAL

- To the north.
- Trace the double pentagram in the air and at the same time vibrate the words of power:

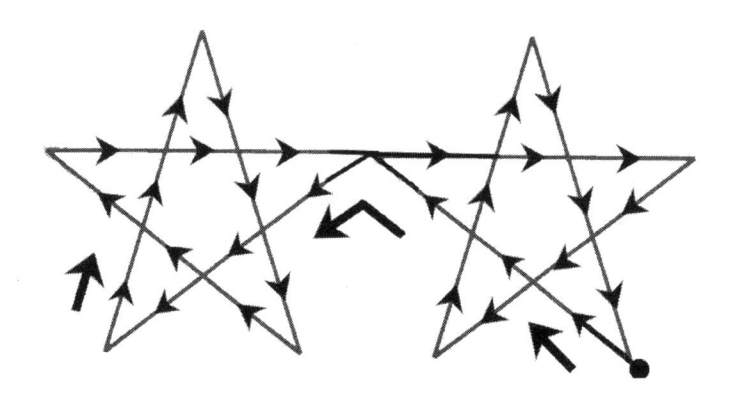

NAHAWAH KABIH OHAN DIATH SHIIBHA NOIIBHA BHAHAN

> Draw the portal clockwise and leave the south side of the portal open.

➢ Place **CEDAR** incense in the center of the circle and a **BLACK** candle inside the portal at the north end. Then light them.
➢ Finish the drawing by closing the portal.

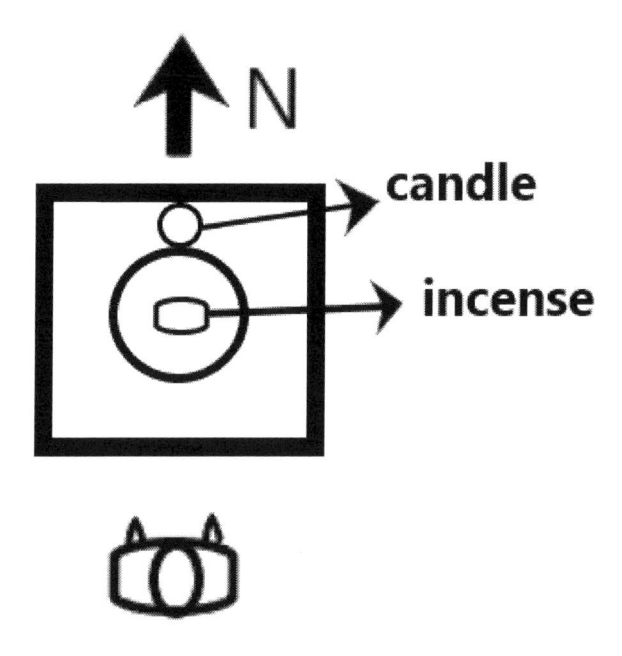

➤ Turn off the light.

➤ Pierce your finger and place 1 drop of blood inside the inner circle
➤ wait a few seconds

➢ Standing with your hands close to your body, recite the invitation:

"KANIBHA HUABHI NANABHI THANIBHA HASHIBHU BANIBHU"

➢ Aguarde alguns segundos em silêncio.

➢ Desenhe a chave no ar diante do portal.

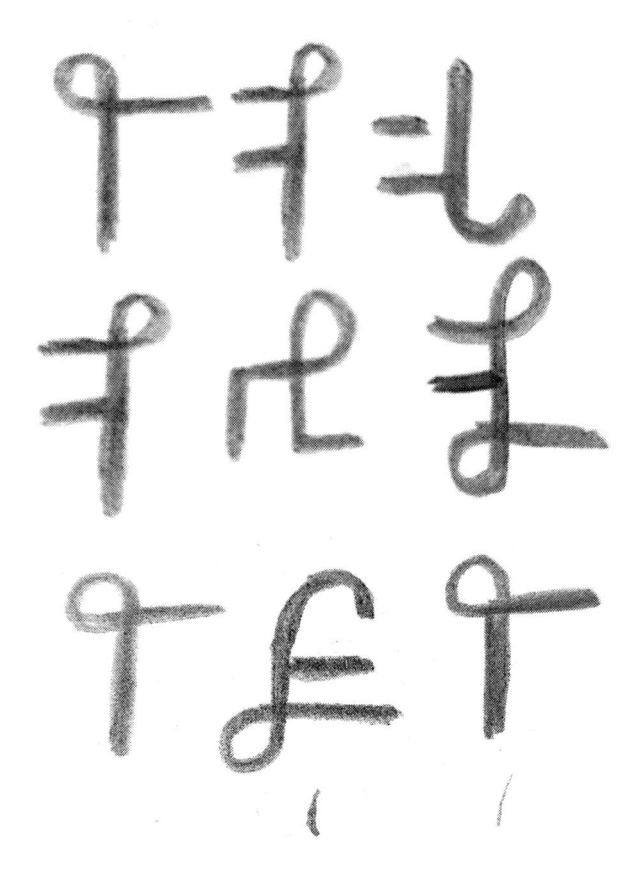

> Wait a few seconds.

> Now recite the evocation 3 times:

"KIV CHRISNONBH KARANA THANIBHA SHORANA PAMDARAH"

- Wait a few minutes and if you don't feel Chrisnonbh's presence repeat the above evocation 3 more times.
- Wait a few minutes.

- If Chrisnonbh has not yet manifested, recite the second evocation 3 times.

"RIUNA CHRISNONBH RIUNA KOAN NAGARA SHORANA"

- At the end of the third recitation it will be there, whether you feel it or not.
- Throw the piece of paper with your order inside the portal. You can write the request on paper before or at this time of the ritual, in Chrisnonbh's presence.
- Envision the request for at least 5 minutes, imagine your request taking place, feel the emotion.
- After having mentalized, say:

"I am grateful to Chrisnonbh for having heard my call and I am grateful for the request made."

- End the ritual.
- Trace the double pentagram in the air and at the same time vibrate the words of power:

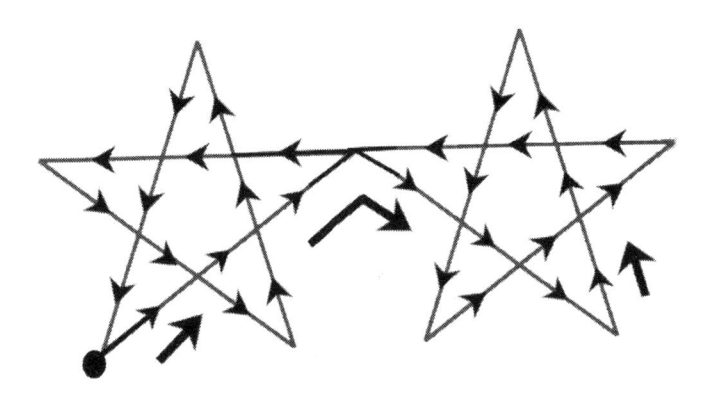

NAHAWAI NOHONAI NAMAHA NAMENIHI KOAN BHALIHI

- Leave the room and let the candle and incense burn to the end.
- Come back 24 hours later to clean everything up.
- Get back to your normal routine and wait for the results of the ritual without anxiety or doubt.

Thimuel

SPECIALTIES

- Attract wealth indirectly through gifts and coincidences.

- Convincing an individual to generously include you in their inheritance.
- To reveal hidden enemies.
- Making enemies take financial losses.

GOETIA

- Corresponds to Valac.

RITUAL

- To the north.
- Trace the double pentagram in the air and at the same time vibrate the words of power:
-

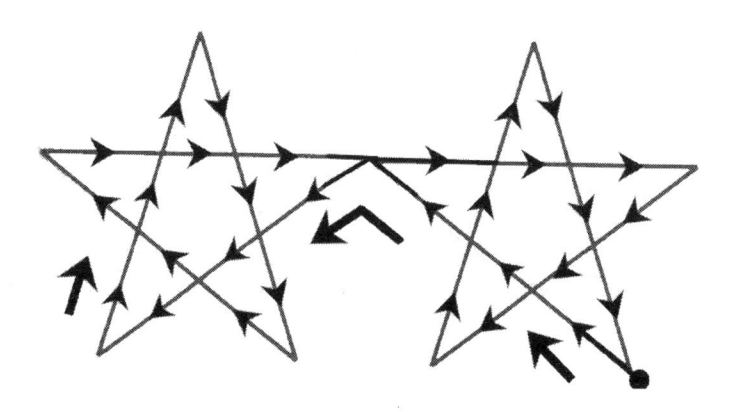

NAHAWAH KABIH OHAN DIATH SHIIBHA NOIIBHA BHAHAN

➢ Draw the portal clockwise and leave the south side of the portal open.

- Place the **ROSES** incense in the center of the circle and a **BLACK** candle inside the portal at the north end. Then light them.
- Finish the drawing by closing the portal.

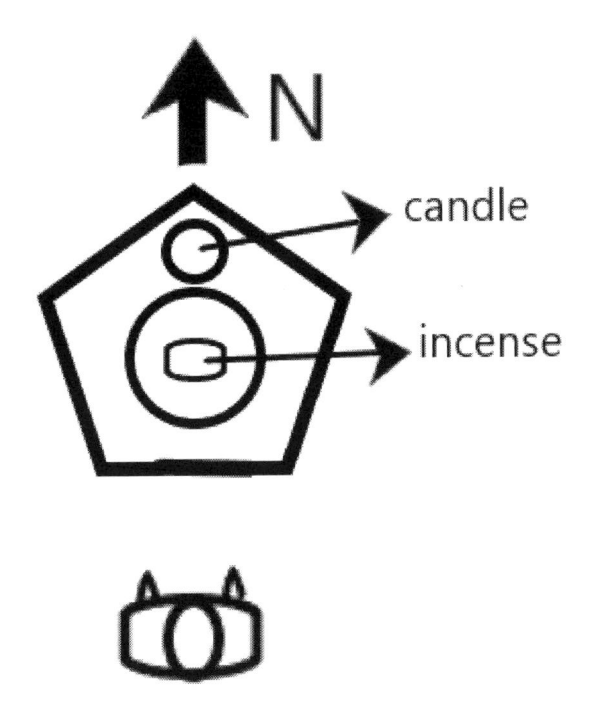

- Turn off the light.

- Pierce your finger and place 1 drop of blood inside the inner circle
- wait a few seconds

- Standing with your hands close to your body, recite the invitation:

"KANIBHA THANIBHA HUABHI DIATH NANABHI HASHIBHU"

- Wait a few seconds in silence.

- Draw the key in the air in front of the portal.

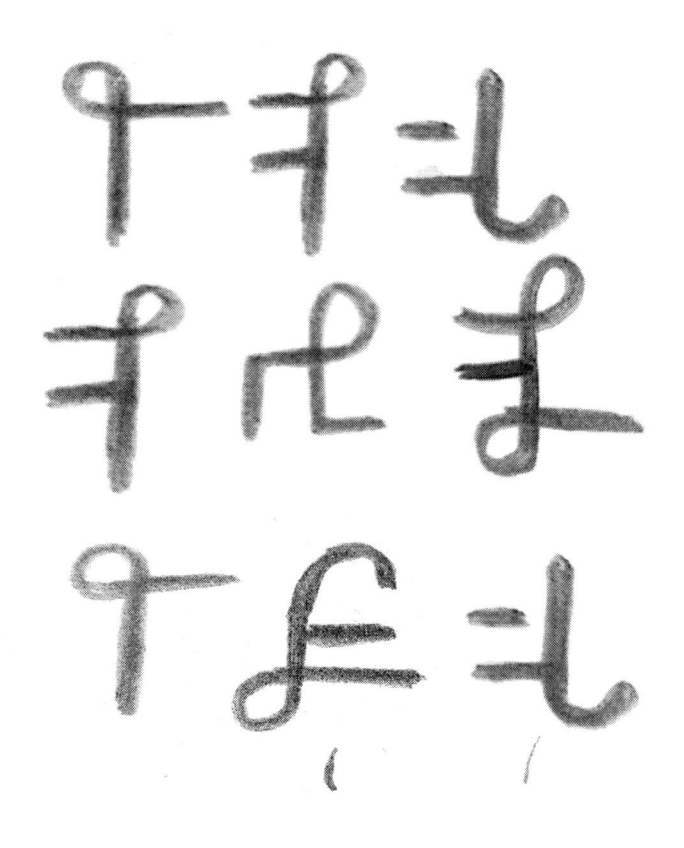

> Wait a few seconds.

> Now recite the evocation 3 times:

"OHAN THIMUEL KARANA RIUNA BANIBHU SHORANA PAMDARAH"

- ➢ Wait a few minutes and if you don't feel Thimuel's presence repeat the above evocation 3 more times.
- ➢ Wait a few minutes.

- ➢ If Thimuel has not yet manifested, recite the second evocation 3 times.

"THIMUEL RIUNA KOAN NAGARA DIATH SHIIBHA SHIBOM"

- ➢ At the end of the third recitation it will be there, whether you feel it or not.
- ➢ Throw the piece of paper with your order inside the portal. You can write the request on paper before or at this time of the ritual, in the presence of Thimuel.
- ➢ Mind the request for at least 5 minutes, imagine your request being carried out, feel the emotion.
- ➢ After having mentalized, say:

"I am grateful to Thimuel for having heard my call and I am grateful for the request made."

- ➢ End the ritual.
- ➢ Trace the double pentagram in the air and at the same time vibrate the words of power:

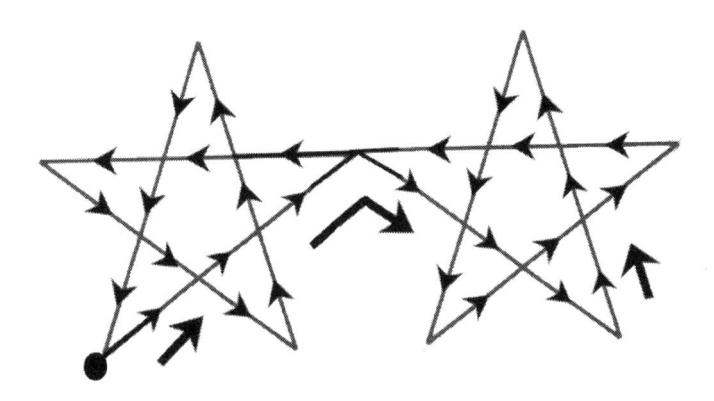

NAHAWAI NOHONAI NAMAHA NAMENIHI KOAN BHALIHI

- ➢ Leave the room and let the candle and incense burn to the end.
- ➢ Come back 24 hours later to clean everything up.
- ➢ Get back to your normal routine and wait for the results of the ritual without anxiety or doubt.

Kuombho

SPECIALTIES

- Success in tests.
- Increased focus.
- Increase knowledge quickly.
- Increase cognition.
- Defeat enemy in humiliating way.
- Humiliate enemy.
- Escape the enemy's trap.

GOETIA

- Corresponds to Asmoday.

RITUAL

- To the north.
- Trace the double pentagram in the air and at the same time vibrate the words of power:

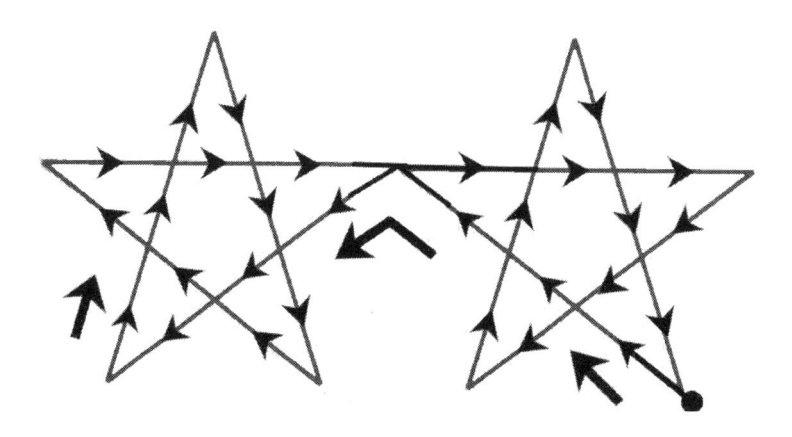

**NAHAWAH KABIH OHAN DIATH SHIIBHA
NOIIBHA BHAHAN**

➢ Draw the portal clockwise and leave the south side of the portal open.

- Place the **MINT** incense in the center of the circle and a **WHITE** or **BLACK** candle inside the outer drawing at the north end. Then light them up.
- Finish the drawing by closing the portal.

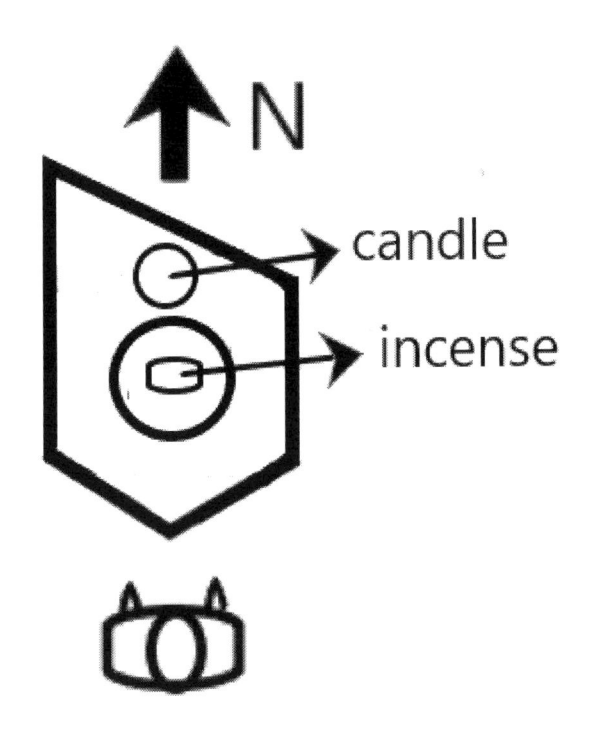

- Turn off the light.
- Standing with your hands at your sides, recite the invitation:

"HUASH SHIAN DANAI NANAHI HUAN"

- Wait a few seconds in silence.
- Draw the key in the air in front of the portal.

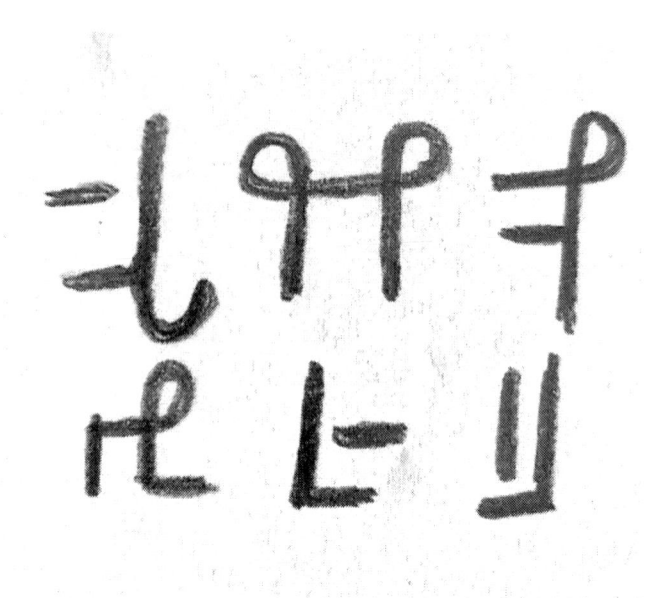

- Wait a few seconds.
- Now recite the evocation 3 times:

"DANAI KONAHAMA ASKVI NANAHI KUOMBHO"

- Wait a few minutes and if you do not feel the presence of Kuombho repeat the above evocation 3 more times.
- Wait a few minutes.
- If Kuombho has not yet spoken, recite the second evocation 3 times.

"RIUNA KONAHAMA SHIRIBHA NANAHI KUOMBHO"

- At the end of the third recitation it will be there, whether you feel it or not.
- Throw the piece of paper with your order into the portal. You can write the request on paper before or at that moment of the ritual, in the presence of Kuombho.
- Mentalize the order for a minimum of 5 minutes, imagine your order being fulfilled, feel the emotion.
- After you have mentalized, say:

"I am grateful to Kuombho for having heard my call and I am grateful for the request made."

- End the ritual.
- Trace the double pentagram in the air and at the same time vibrate the words of power:

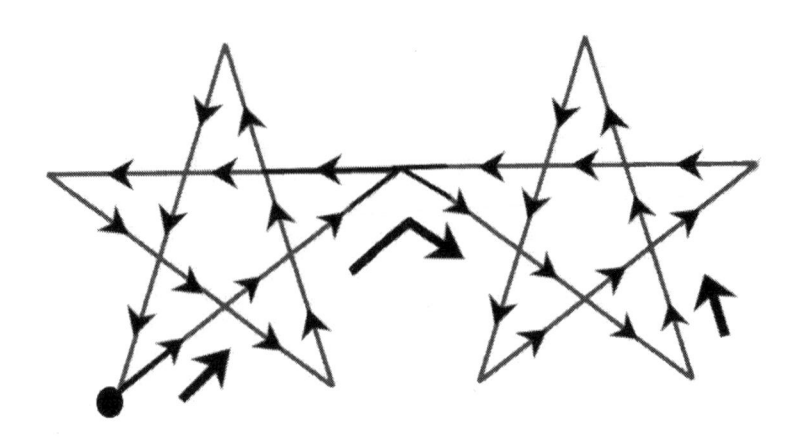

NAHAWAI NOHONAI NAMAHA NAMENIHI KOAN BHALIHI

- ➢ Exit the room and let the candle and incense burn to the end.
- ➢ Come back 24 hours later to clean up.
- ➢ Go back to your normal routine and wait for the results of the ritual without anxiety or doubt.

Odhinga

SPECIALTIES

- Create discord between two named individuals.

- Create discord, mistrust and jealousy within a group.
- Create distrust, fear and hatred in a group against its leader.
- modify the future
- Make everyone agree with your opinion
- Achieve material goods.

GOETIA

- It corresponds to Andras.

RITUAL

- To the north.
- Trace the double pentagram in the air and at the same time vibrate the words of power:

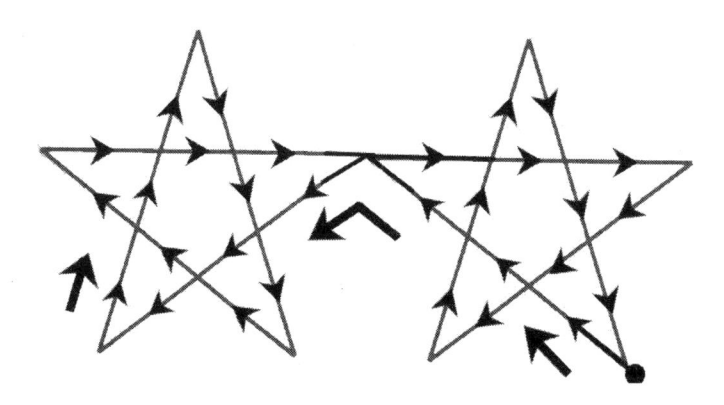

**NAHAWAH KABIH OHAN DIATH SHIIBHA
NOIIBHA BHAHAN**

➢ Draw the portal clockwise and leave the south side of the portal open.

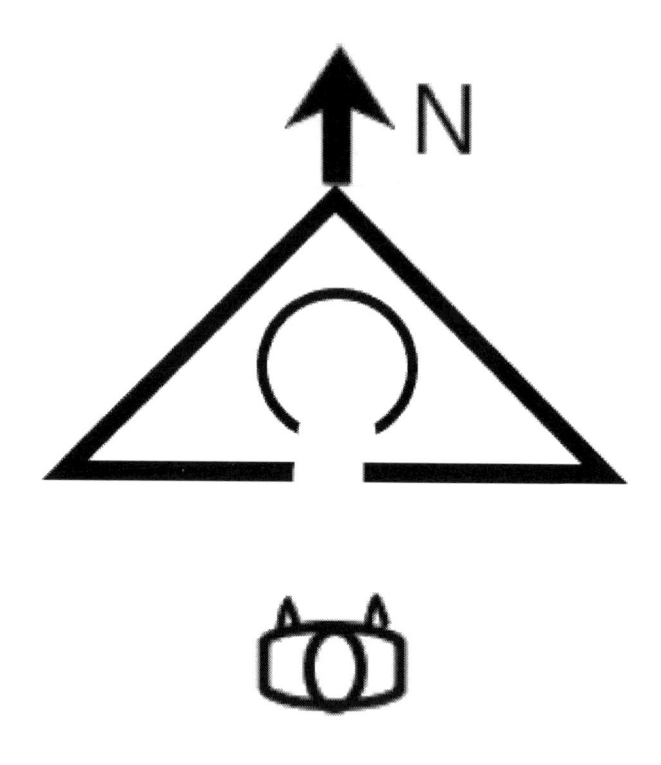

➢ Place the **ROSEMARY** incense in the center of the circle and a **BLACK** candle inside the portal at the north end. Then light them.
➢ Finish the drawing by closing the portal.

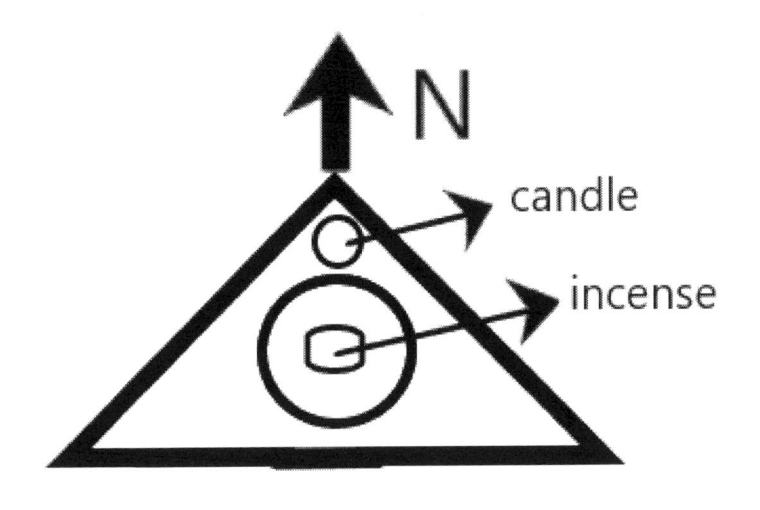

- Turn off the light.

- Pierce your finger and place 1 drop of blood inside the inner circle
- wait a few seconds

➢ Standing with your hands close to your body, recite the invitation:

"KANIBHA THANIBHA HUABHI NANABHI HASHIBHU BANIBHU"

➢ Wait a few seconds in silence.

➢ Draw the key in the air in front of the portal.

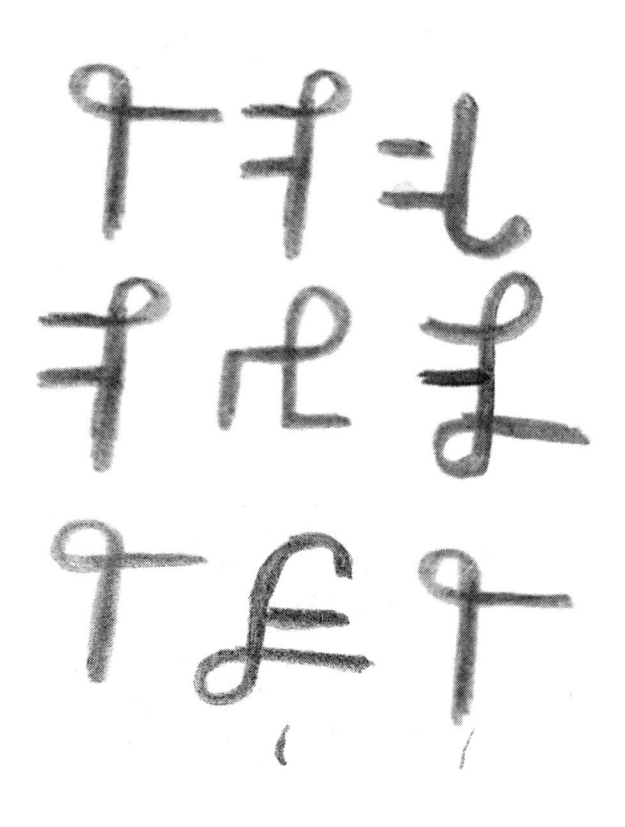

- Wait a few seconds.

- Now recite the evocation 3 times:

"KABIH OHAN KARANA RIUNA ODHINGA SHORANA KOAN"

- Wait a few minutes and if you don't feel the presence of Odhinga repeat the above evocation 3 more times.
- Wait a few minutes.

- If Odhinga has not yet manifested, recite the second evocation 3 times.

"HUABHI ODHINGA NANABHI RIUNA KOAN NAGARA SHIBOM"

- At the end of the third recitation it will be there, whether you feel it or not.
- Throw the piece of paper with your order inside the portal. You can write the request on paper before or at this time of the ritual, in the presence of Odhinga.
- Mind the request for at least 5 minutes, imagine your request being carried out, feel the emotion.
- After having mentalized, say:

"I thank Odhinga for having heard my call and I thank him for the request made."

- End the ritual.
- Trace the double pentagram in the air and at the same time vibrate the words of power:

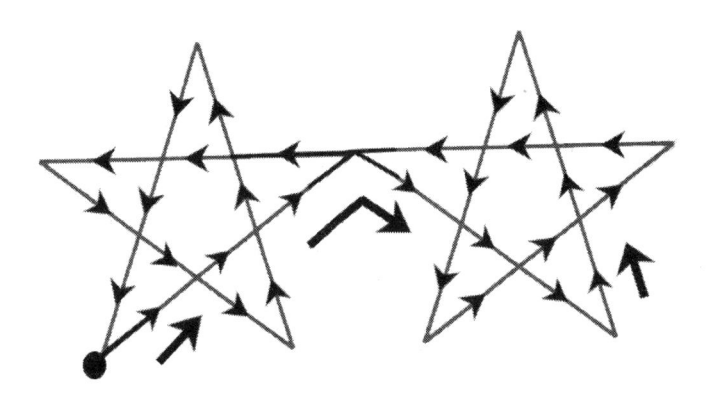

NAHAWAI NOHONAI NAMAHA NAMENIHI KOAN BHALIHI

- Saia do recinto e deixe a vela e o incenso queimarem até o fim.
- Volte 24 horas depois para limpar tudo.
- Volte a sua rotina normal e aguarde os resultados do ritual sem ansiedade ou dúvida.

Nebhituagh

SPECIALTIES

- Manipulate an individual's thoughts.
- To gain insight into an individual's thoughts.
- To increase your ability to make people give you free money
- close a profitable business
- Making enemies take financial losses.

GOETIA

- Corresponds to Botis.

RITUAL

- To the north.
- Trace the double pentagram in the air and at the same time vibrate the words of power:

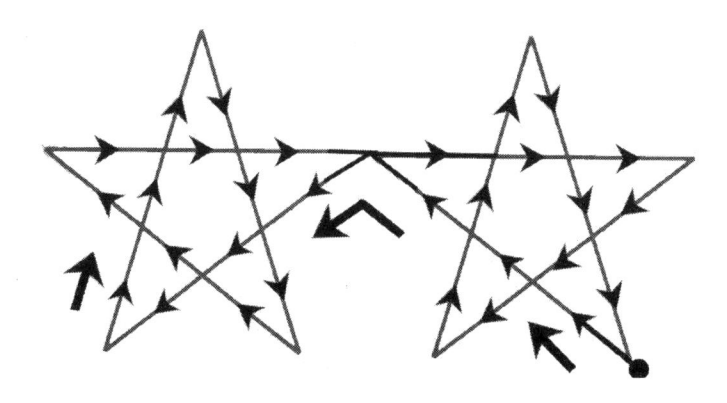

NAHAWAH KABIH OHAN DIATH SHIIBHA NOIIBHA BHAHAN

> Draw the portal clockwise and leave the south side of the portal open.

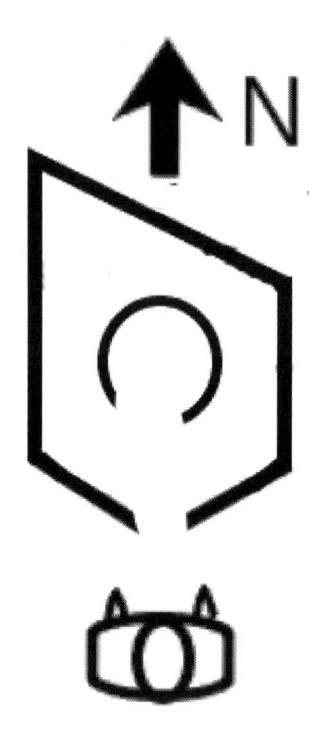

➢ Place the **PALO SANTO** incense in the center of the circle and a **BLACK** or **BLUE** candle inside the square at the north end. Then light them.
➢ Finish the drawing by closing the portal.

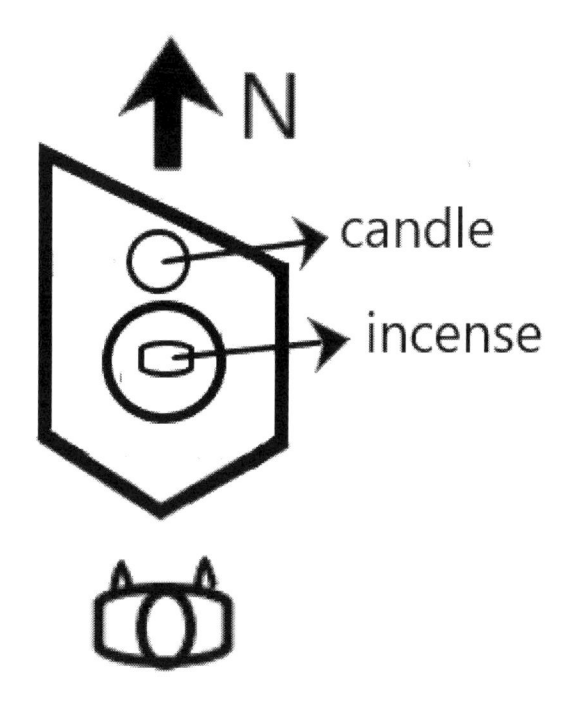

➢ Turn off the light.

➢ Pierce your finger and place 1 drop of blood inside the inner circle
➢ wait a few seconds

- Standing with your hands close to your body, recite the invitation:

"KANIBHA THANIBHA HANABHI NANABHI HASHIBHU BANIBHU"

- Wait a few seconds in silence.

- Draw the key in the air in front of the portal.

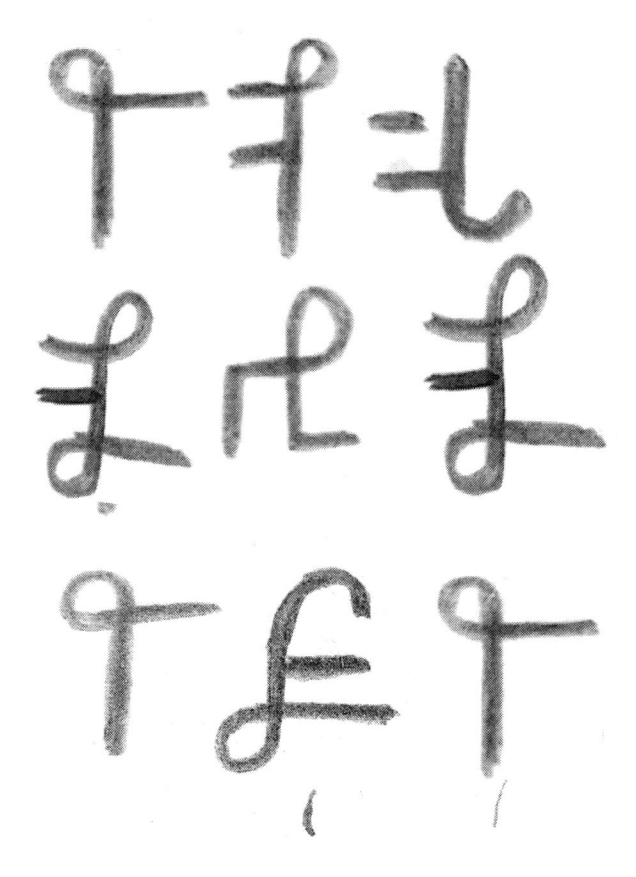

➢ Wait a few seconds.

➢ Now recite the evocation 3 times:

"PARAN NEBHITUAGH HUABHI NANABHI RIUNA SHORANA PARAH"

- Wait a few minutes and if you don't feel Nebhituagh's presence repeat the above evocation 3 more times.
- Wait a few minutes.

- If Nebhituagh has not yet manifested, recite the second evocation 3 times.

"NEBHITUAGH RIUNA HUABHI NAGARA SHORANA PARAN"

- At the end of the third recitation it will be there, whether you feel it or not.
- Throw the piece of paper with your order inside the portal. You can write the request on paper before or at this time of the ritual, in the presence of Nebhituagh.
- Envision the request for at least 5 minutes, imagine your request taking place, feel the emotion.
- After having mentalized, say:

"I thank Nebhituagh for having heard my call and thank you for the request made."

- ➢ End the ritual.
- ➢ Trace the double pentagram in the air and at the same time vibrate the words of power:

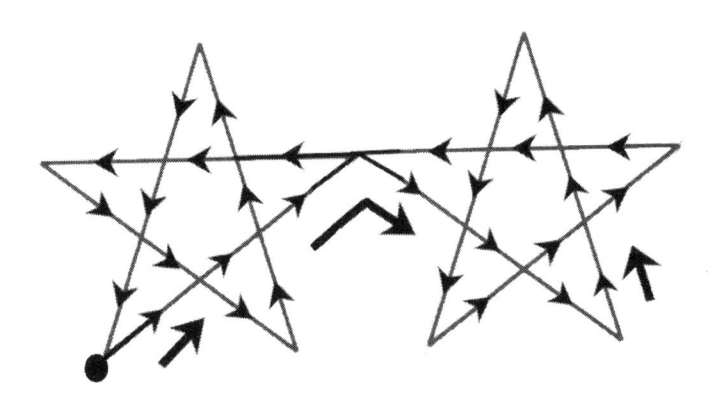

NAHAWAI NOHONAI NAMAHA NAMENIHI KOAN BHALIHI

- ➢ Leave the room and let the candle and incense burn to the end.
- ➢ Come back 24 hours later to clean everything up.
- ➢ Get back to your normal routine and wait for the results of the ritual without anxiety or doubt.

Nirondhi

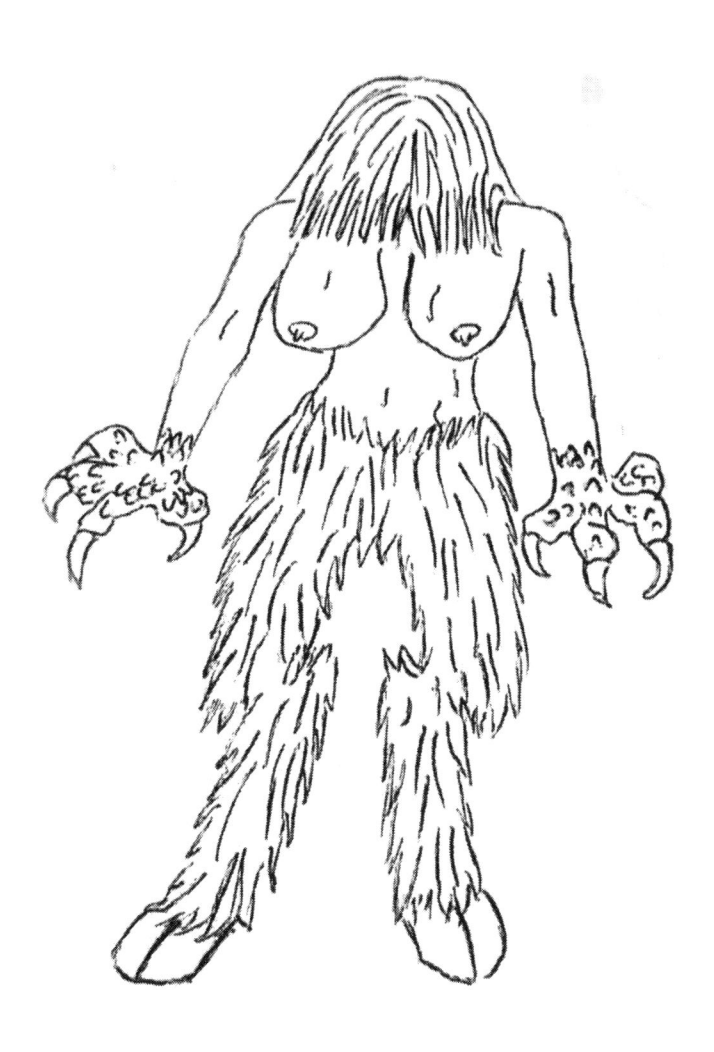

SPECIALTIES

- Take your enemy's strength and bring it to you
- Take money from your enemy and bring it to you
- Making enemies take financial losses.
- bankrupt enemy
- Inflicting leprosy on an enemy.

GOETIA

- It corresponds to Malphas.

RITUAL

- To the north.
- Trace the double pentagram in the air and at the same time vibrate the words of power:

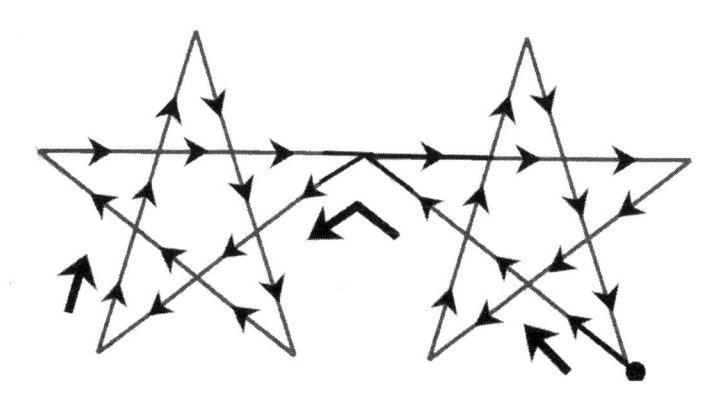

NAHAWAH KABIH OHAN DIATH SHIIBHA NOIIBHA BHAHAN

- Draw the portal clockwise and leave the south side of the portal open.

- Place **SAGE** incense in the center of the circle and a **WHITE** or **BLACK** candle inside the portal at the north end. Then light them.
- Finish the drawing by closing the portal.

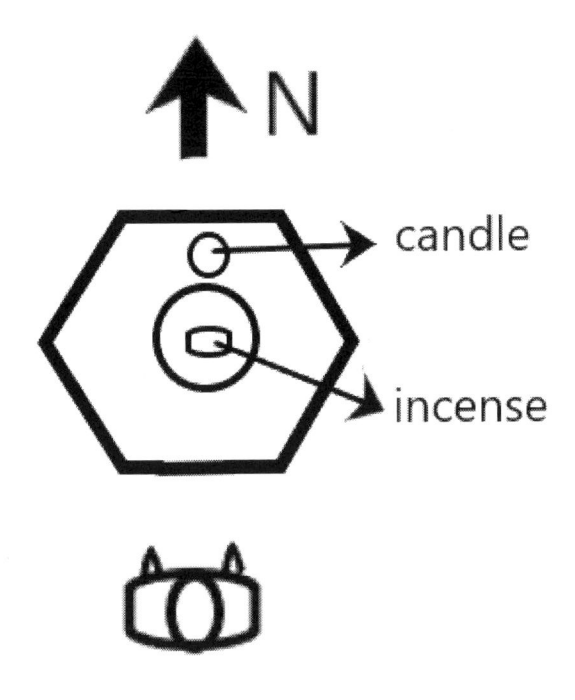

➢ Turn off the light.

➢ Pierce your finger and place 1 drop of blood inside the inner circle
➢ wait a few seconds

➢ Standing with your hands close to your body, recite the invitation:

"KANIBHA THANIBHA HUABHI NAGARA HASHIBHU BANIBHU"

➢ Wait a few seconds in silence.

➢ Draw the key in the air in front of the portal.

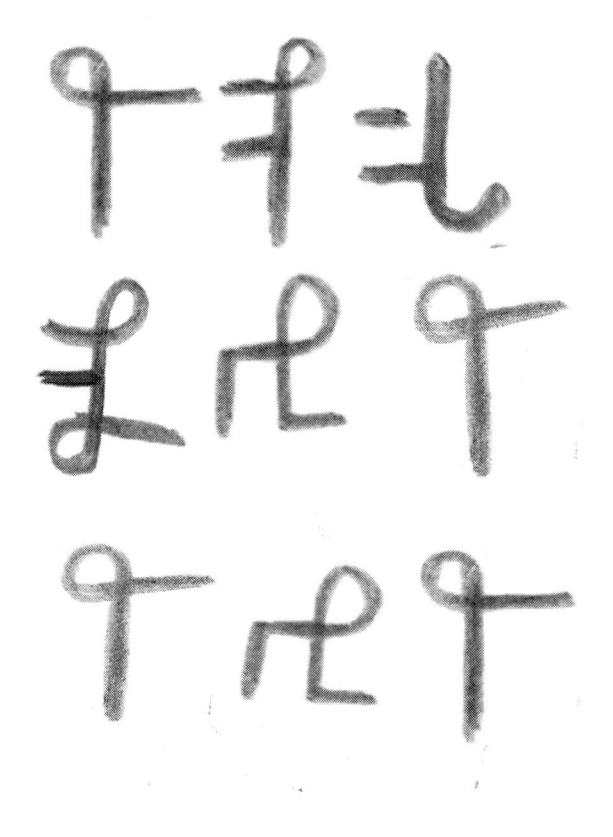

➤ Wait a few seconds.

➤ Now recite the evocation 3 times:

"NIRONDHI THANIBHA KIV KARANA RIUNA SHORANA PAMDARAH"

- Wait a few minutes and if you don't feel Nirondhi's presence repeat the above evocation 3 more times.
- Wait a few minutes.

- If Nirondhi has not yet manifested, recite the second evocation 3 times.

"NIRONDHI RIUNA THANIBHA KOAN NANABHI KABIH SHIBOM"

- At the end of the third recitation it will be there, whether you feel it or not.
- Throw the piece of paper with your order inside the portal. You can write the request on paper before or at this time of the ritual, in Nirondhi's presence.
- Envision the request for at least 5 minutes, imagine your request taking place, feel the emotion.
- After having mentalized, say:

"I thank Nirondhi for having heard my call and I thank him for the request made."

- ➢ End the ritual.
- ➢ Trace the double pentagram in the air and at the same time vibrate the words of power:

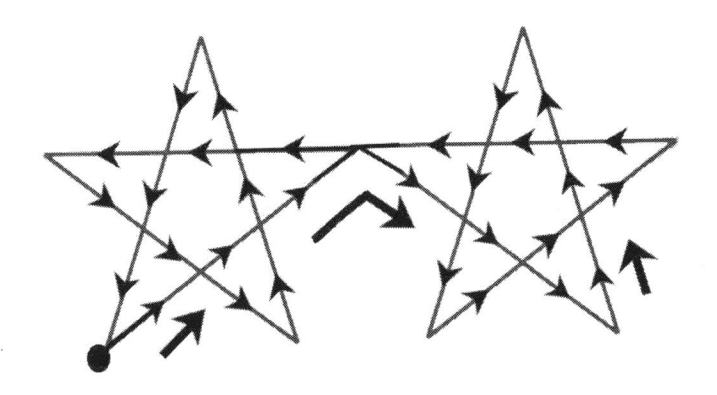

NAHAWAI NOHONAI NAMAHA NAMENIHI KOAN BHALIHI

- ➢ Leave the room and let the candle and incense burn to the end.
- ➢ Come back 24 hours later to clean everything up.
- ➢ Get back to your normal routine and wait for the results of the ritual without anxiety or doubt.

Bhaldondhi

SPECIALTIES

- Strengthen your willpower while increasing your money
- Remove limiting beliefs from your subconscious
- Strengthen a thriving mindset.
- Putting you in a leadership role
- Bring discouragement to your enemy

GOETIA

- It corresponds to Halphas.

RITUAL

- To the north.
- Trace the double pentagram in the air and at the same time vibrate the words of power:

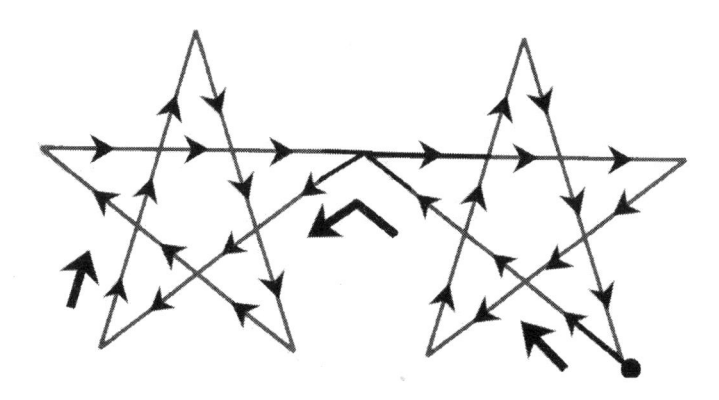

NAHAWAH KABIH OHAN DIATH SHIIBHA NOIIBHA BHAHAN

- Draw the portal clockwise and leave the south side of the portal open.

- ➤ Place **SAGE** incense in the center of the circle and a **WHITE** or **BLACK** candle inside the Portal at the north end. Then light them.
- ➤ Finish the drawing by closing the portal.

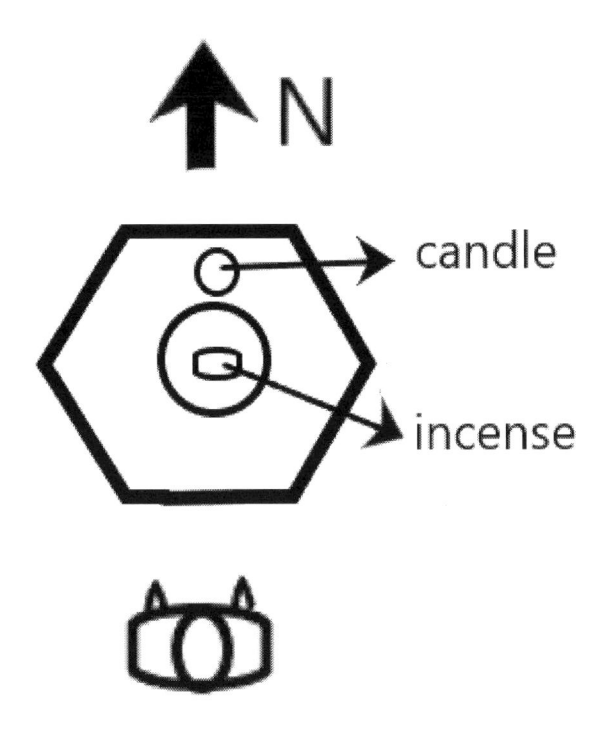

- Turn off the light.

- Pierce your finger and place 1 drop of blood inside the inner circle
- wait a few seconds

305

➢ Standing with your hands close to your body, recite the invitation:

"KANIBHA HUABHI NANABHI HASHIBHU BANIBHA THANIBHA"

➢ Wait a few seconds in silence.

➢ Draw the key in the air in front of the portal.

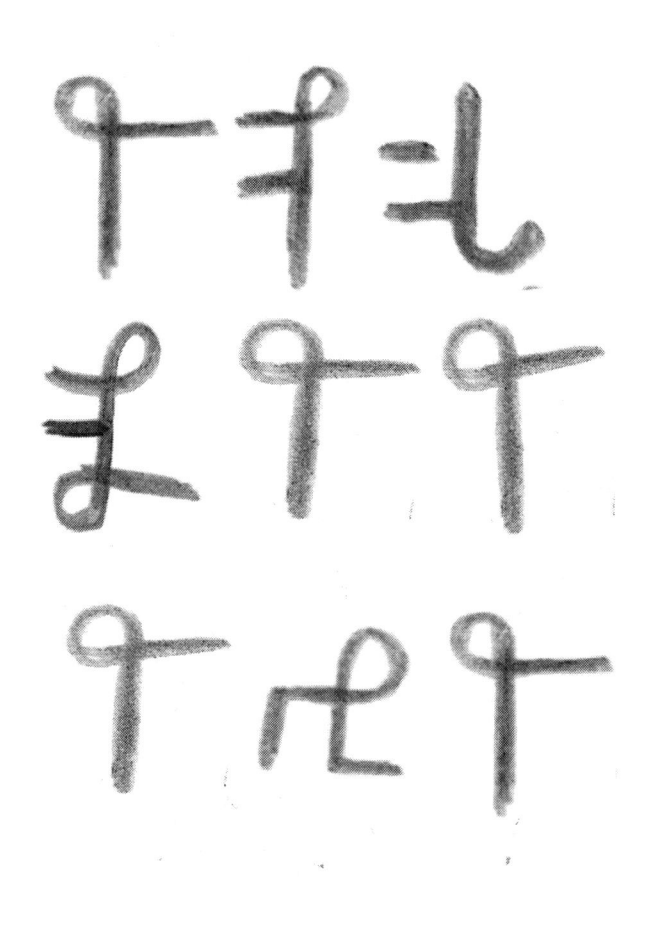

➢ Wait a few seconds.

➢ Now recite the evocation 3 times:

"THANIBHA BHALDONDHI KARANA SHORANA PAMDARAH KASHID"

- Wait a few minutes and if you don't feel Bhaldondhi's presence repeat the above evocation 3 more times.
- Wait a few minutes.

- If Bhaldondhi has not yet manifested, recite the second evocation 3 times.

"BHALDONDHI RIUNA KOAN NAGARA SHORANA NANABHI SHIBOM"

- At the end of the third recitation it will be there, whether you feel it or not.
- Throw the piece of paper with your order inside the portal. You can write the request on paper before or at this time of the ritual, in the presence of Bhaldondhi.
- Mind the request for at least 5 minutes, imagine your request being carried out, feel the emotion.
- After having mentalized, say:

"I thank Bhaldondhi for having heard my call and I thank him for carrying out my request."

- ➢ End the ritual.
- ➢ Trace the double pentagram in the air and at the same time vibrate the words of power:

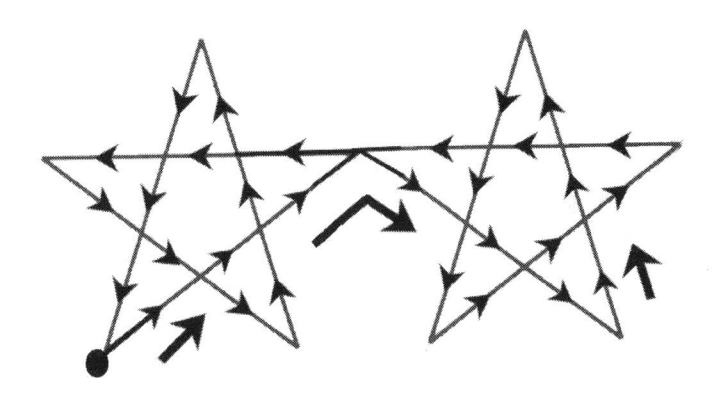

NAHAWAI NOHONAI NAMAHA NAMENIHI KOAN BHALIHI

- ➢ Leave the room and let the candle and incense burn to the end.
- ➢ Come back 24 hours later to clean everything up.
- ➢ Get back to your normal routine and wait for the results of the ritual without anxiety or doubt.

Yanklauthemar

SPECIALTIES

- Bringing money through art and culture
- Generate wealth through trade
- Reveal gold and gemstones.
- bankrupt your enemy quickly

GOETIA

- Corresponds to Paimon.

RITUAL

- To the north.
- Trace the double pentagram in the air and at the same time vibrate the words of power:

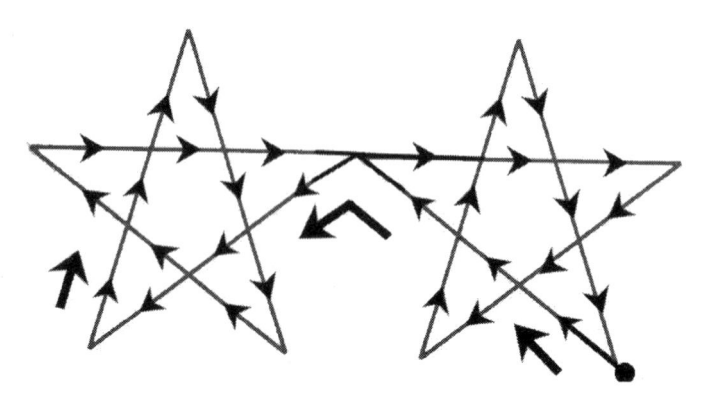

NAHAWAH KABIH OHAN DIATH SHIIBHA NOIIBHA BHAHAN

- Draw the portal clockwise and leave the south side of the portal open.

- ➢ Place the **MINT** incense in the center of the circle and a **BLACK** or **YELLOW** candle inside the portal at the north end. Then light them.
- ➢ Finish the drawing by closing the portal.

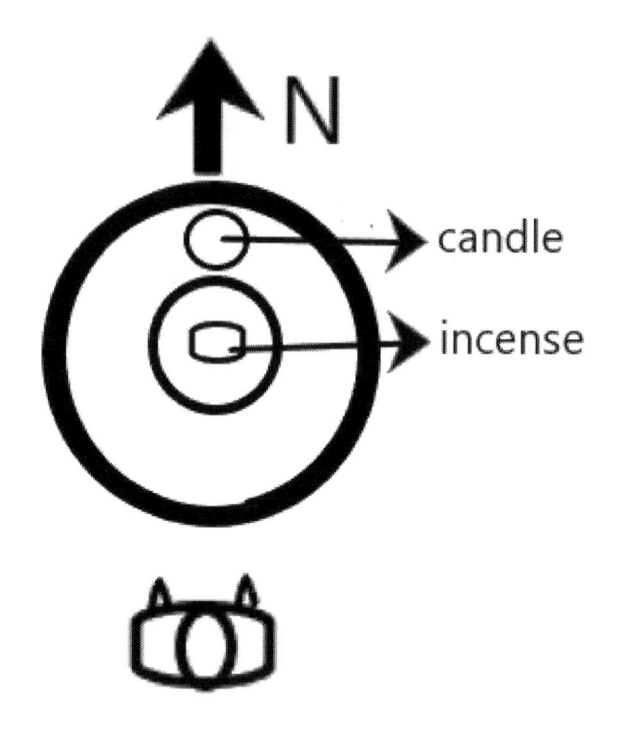

➤ Turn off the light.

➤ Pierce your finger and place 1 drop of blood inside the inner circle
➤ wait a few seconds

➢ Standing with your hands close to your body, recite the invitation:

"KANIBHA THANIBHA HUABHI NANABHI HASHIBHU BANIBHU"

➢ Wait a few seconds in silence.

➢ Draw the key in the air in front of the portal.

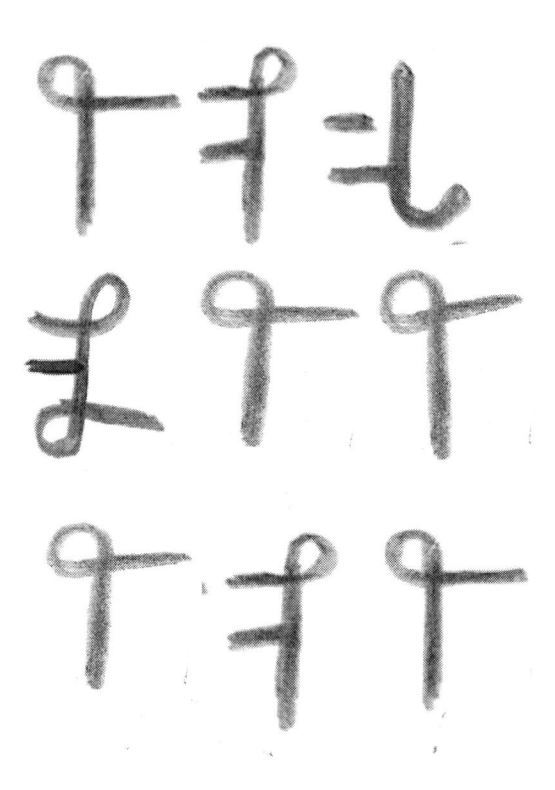

- Wait a few seconds.

- Now recite the evocation 3 times:

"SHIIBHA KARANA YANKLAUTHEMAR RIUNA THANIBHA SHORANA NAHAWAH"

- Wait a few minutes and if you don't feel Yanklauthemar's presence, repeat the above evocation 3 more times.
- Wait a few minutes.

- If Yanklauthemar has not yet manifested, recite the second evocation 3 times.

"NAMASH YANKLAUTHEMAR THANIBHA KOAN NAGARA SHORANA"

- At the end of the third recitation it will be there, whether you feel it or not.
- Throw the piece of paper with your order inside the portal. You can write the request on

paper before or at this time of the ritual, in Yanklauthemar's presence.
- ➤ Mind the request for at least 5 minutes, imagine your request being carried out, feel the emotion.
- ➤ After having mentalized, say:

"I thank Yanklauthemar for listening to my call and thank him for carrying out my order."

- ➤ End the ritual.
- ➤ Trace the double pentagram in the air and at the same time vibrate the words of power:

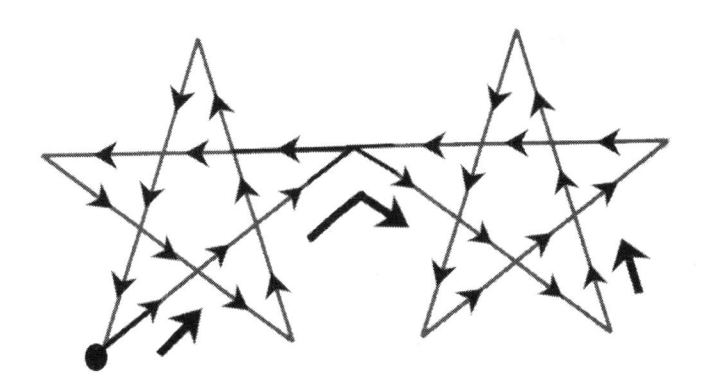

NAHAWAI NOHONAI NAMAHA NAMENIHI KOAN BHALIHI

- Leave the room and let the candle and incense burn to the end.
- Come back 24 hours later to clean everything up.
- Get back to your normal routine and wait for the results of the ritual without anxiety or doubt.

Maranghonebhiros

SPECIALTIES

- ➢ Bring unexpected cash
- ➢ Bring good fame
- ➢ Bring victory in games of chance
- ➢ Make enemy lose money.

GOETIA

- ➢ It corresponds to Barbatos.

RITUAL

- ➢ To the north.
- ➢ Trace the double pentagram in the air and at the same time vibrate the words of power:

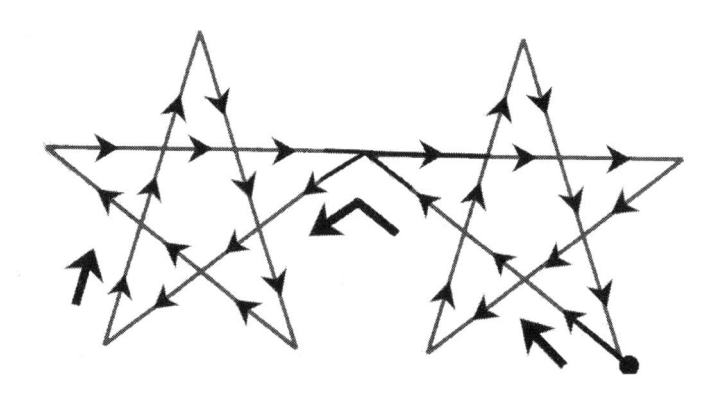

NAHAWAH KABIH OHAN DIATH SHIIBHA NOIIBHA BHAHAN

➤ Draw the portal clockwise and leave the south side of the portal open.

- Place the **ROSES** incense in the center of the circle and a **BLACK** or **ORANGE** candle inside the portal at the north end. Then light them.
- Finish the drawing by closing the portal.

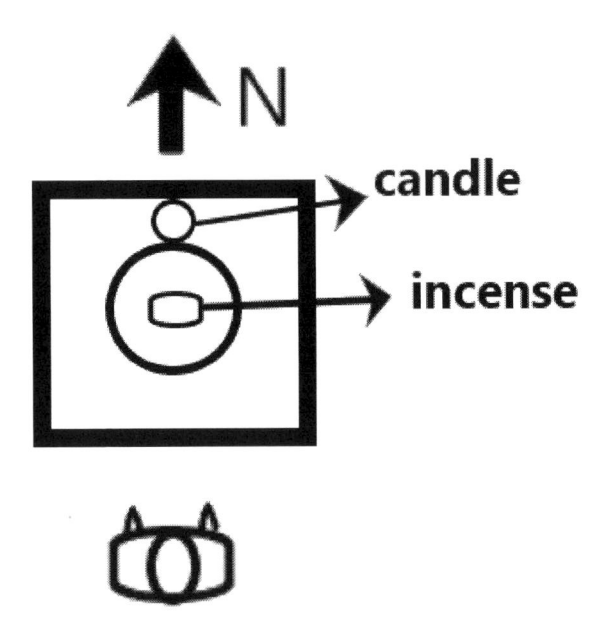

- Turn off the light.

- Pierce your finger and place 1 drop of blood inside the inner circle
- wait a few seconds

- Standing with your hands close to your body, recite the invitation:

"KANIBHA THANIBHA HUABHI NOIIBHA HASHIBHU BANIBHU"

> Wait a few seconds in silence.

> Draw the key in the air in front of the portal.

> Wait a few seconds.

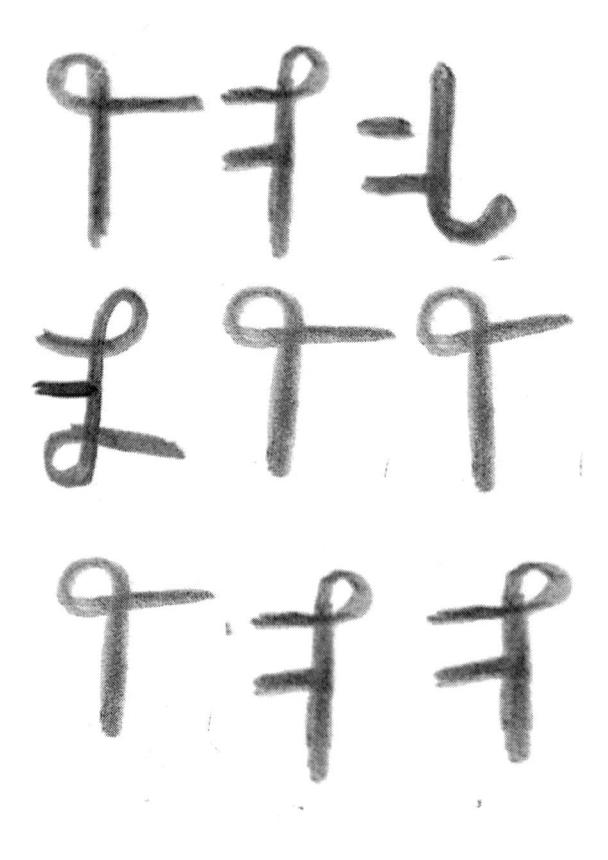

- Now recite the evocation 3 times:

"KIV MARANGHONEBHIROS NANABHI KARANA RIUNA HASHIBHU SHORANA PAMDARAH"

- Wait a few minutes and if you don't feel the presence of Maranghonebhiros repeat the above evocation 3 more times.
- Wait a few minutes.

- If Maranghonebhiros has not yet manifested, recite the second evocation 3 times.

"KIV MARANGHONEBHIROS RIUNA KOAN NANABHI HASHIBHU"

- At the end of the third recitation it will be there, whether you feel it or not.
- Throw the piece of paper with your order inside the portal. You can write the request on paper before or at this time of the ritual, in the presence of Maranghonebhiros.

- Mind the request for at least 5 minutes, imagine your request being carried out, feel the emotion.
- After having mentalized, say:

"I thank Maranghonebhiros for having heeded my call and I thank him for carrying out my request."

- End the ritual.
- Trace the double pentagram in the air and at the same time vibrate the words of power:

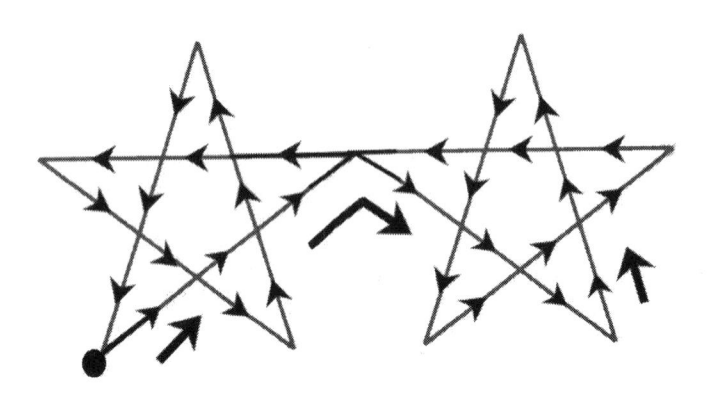

NAHAWAI NOHONAI NAMAHA NAMENIHI KOAN BHALIHI

- Leave the room and let the candle and incense burn to the end.

- Come back 24 hours later to clean everything up.
- Get back to your normal routine and wait for the results of the ritual without anxiety or doubt.

Thedhiongharitha

SPECIALTIES

- Make it easier to master several languages
- facilitate the study
- Create opportunity to earn money from your expertise
- attract a good job

- Attract a partner with great wealth.

GOETIA

- It corresponds to Crocell.

RITUAL

- To the north.
- Trace the double pentagram in the air and at the same time vibrate the words of power:

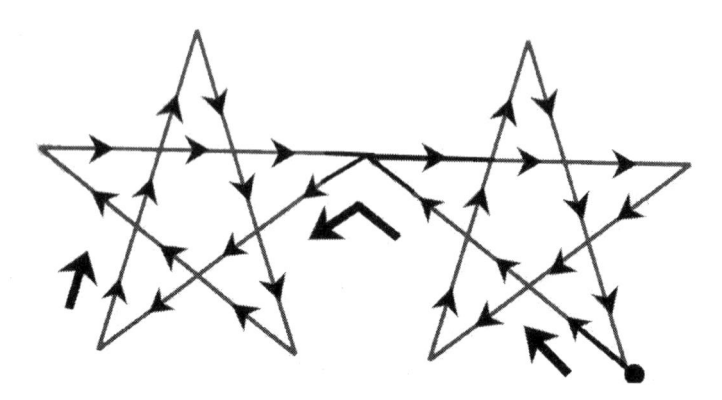

NAHAWAH KABIH OHAN DIATH SHIIBHA NOIIBHA BHAHAN

➤ Draw the portal clockwise and leave the south side of the portal open.

- Place **JASMINE** incense in the center of the circle and a **BLACK** candle inside the portal at the north end. Then light them.
- Finish the drawing by closing the portal.

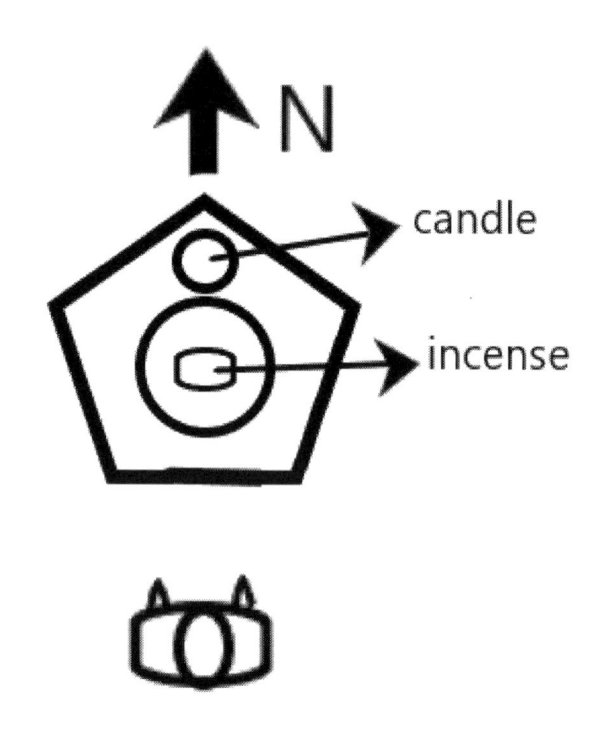

candle

incense

- Turn off the light.

- Pierce your finger and place 1 drop of blood inside the inner circle
- wait a few seconds

- Standing with your hands close to your body, recite the invitation:

"KANIBHA THANIBHA HUABHI NANABHI HASHIBHU BANIBHU"

- Wait a few seconds in silence.

- Draw the key in the air in front of the portal.

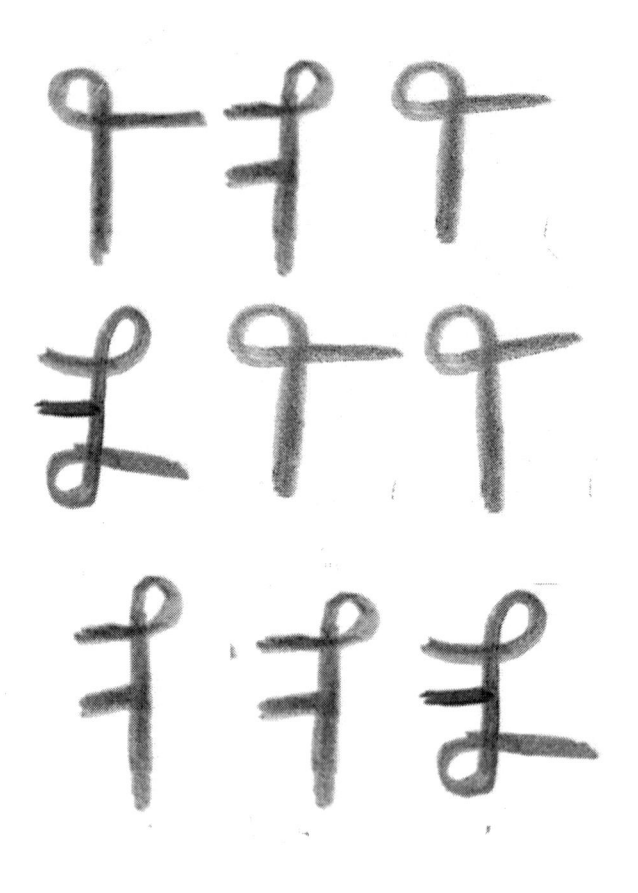

- Wait a few seconds.

- Now recite the evocation 3 times:

"THEDHIONGHARITHA HUABHI KARANA RIUNA NOIIBHA BHAHAN"

- Wait a few minutes and if you don't feel Thedhiongharitha's presence repeat the above evocation 3 more times.
- Wait a few minutes.
- If Thedhiongharitha has not yet manifested, recite the second evocation 3 times.

"THEDHIONGHARITHA NOIIBHA RIUNA BHAHAN NAGARA SHIBOM"

- At the end of the third recitation it will be there, whether you feel it or not.
- Throw the piece of paper with your order inside the portal. You can write the request on paper before or at this time of the ritual, in the presence of Thedhiongharitha.
- Envision the request for at least 5 minutes, imagine your request taking place, feel the emotion.
- After having mentalized, say:

"I thank Thedhiongharitha for having heard my call and thank you for carrying out my request."

- ➤ End the ritual.
- ➤ Trace the double pentagram in the air and at the same time vibrate the words of power:

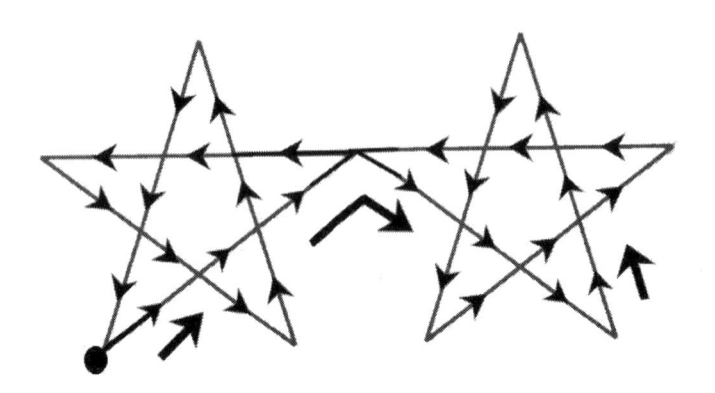

NAHAWAI NOHONAI NAMAHA NAMENIHI KOAN BHALIHI

- ➤ Leave the room and let the candle and incense burn to the end.
- ➤ Come back 24 hours later to clean everything up.
- ➤ Get back to your normal routine and wait for the results of the ritual without anxiety or doubt.

Ritual of Success and Victory with Shamanic Magick

I decided to publish this ritual in this book because it's a ritual that has helped me many times, and it can help you too.

The more people discover Magick and the more positive results magick brings to people's lives, the weaker the Demiurge's power over this world will be.

The less magick there is in a person's life, the greater is "god (jeovah)", and the more magick there is in a person's life, the less "god (jeovah)" becomes. The Demiurge is so small in the life of those who practice Magick that he arrives and disappears. And the true God awakens, you!

Most occult writers and books of practical magick do not reveal their secrets fully and this interferes with the power of magick. I don't believe everything I know can fit in the pages of a book or dozens of books, but everything I've published to date has been in full, all the pieces are there and you just need to turn the first gear that the whole set will start working.

And in this chapter I bring a ritual that is passed orally among the Shamans of my people, for the first time recorded in writing and for the first time published.

This ritual serves to remove all obstacles that keep you from being victorious and successful.

If you obstruct the passage of water in a river, the water will dam in one part of the river and there will be no water for the rest of its length. If that which obstructs the water in the river is removed, the water will naturally flow again.

And that's what this ritual does, it removes the obstructions that keep you from succeeding and winning, and good things will start flowing naturally to you.

The ritual is simple but very powerful, make good use of it.

MATERIALS

- Something to do the drawings on the floor
- 4 black candles.
- 1 picture of you.

RITUAL

- Around midnight
- Preferably on the full moon
- Draw the sigil on the ground in a northerly direction.

- Place a black candle towards each cardinal point.
- Put your photo over the sigil.

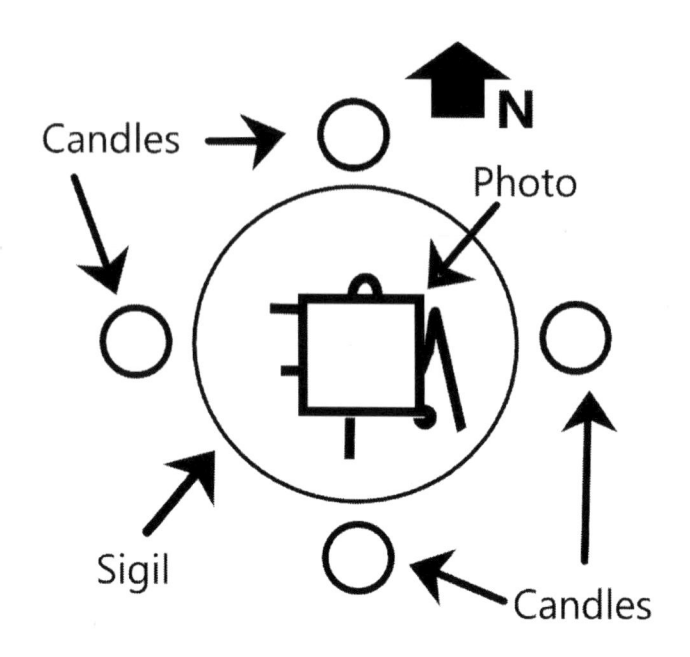

- Light the candles and turn off the light.
- In the face of sigil, say:

"I ask the Gods to energize this sigil and that the energies of the four quadrants of the universe flow through this sigil".

- Wait a few minutes.
- Now call for the Gods:

"I call Dirindho"

> Wait a few seconds.

"I call Noabhind"

> Wait a few seconds.

"I call Hifh"

> Wait a few seconds.

"I call Bhoran"

> Wait a few seconds.

"I call Nathandha"

> Wait a few seconds.

"I call Hanthal"

> Wait a few seconds.

"I call Malentha"

> Wait a few seconds.

"I call Khoril"

> Wait a few seconds.

"I call Dhithupo"

> Wait a few seconds.

"I call Patheo"

> Wait a few seconds.

> Say it:

"I focus the energy of the four quadrants of the universe into this sigil with the support of the Gods of Victory.

Nothing can object to this.

All the power that flows through the sigil now flows through me.

The Gods decreed and so it will be".

- Wait a few minutes in silence.
- Say it:

"I thank the Gods for listening to me and now the path is flat, I can walk without difficulty and get everything I want".

- Let the candles burn to the end.
- Leave the place.

Ritual to Defeat the Enemy with Shamanic Magick

When we least expect it, an inconvenient person appears to mess up our plans, and that's what this ritual is all about.

This is the weapon to put people against your goals in their place, which is below you.

So let's get down to the ritual...

MATERIALS

- 1 black candle
- Your enemy's photo or full name
- 1 large onion

RITUAL

- in a dark night
- facing north
- Say it:

"I call the Lords of War and Death to support my work"

- wait a few seconds
- Make a hole in the center of the onion that goes through it
- Fit the black candle into the hole

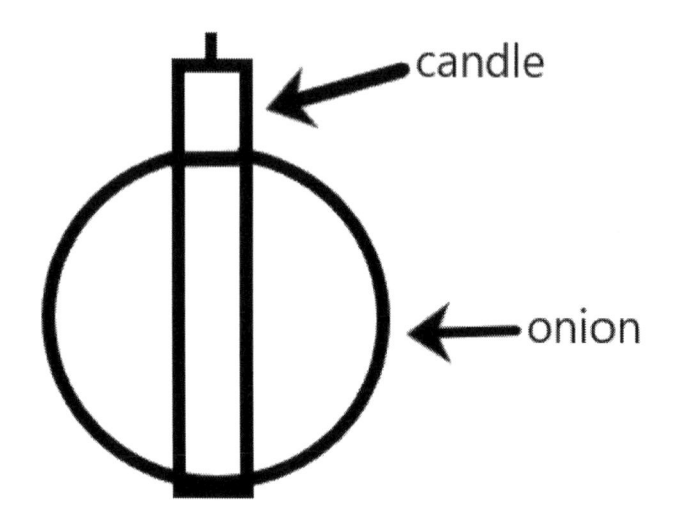

← candle

← onion

- Place the onion with the candle over the enemy's photo or name

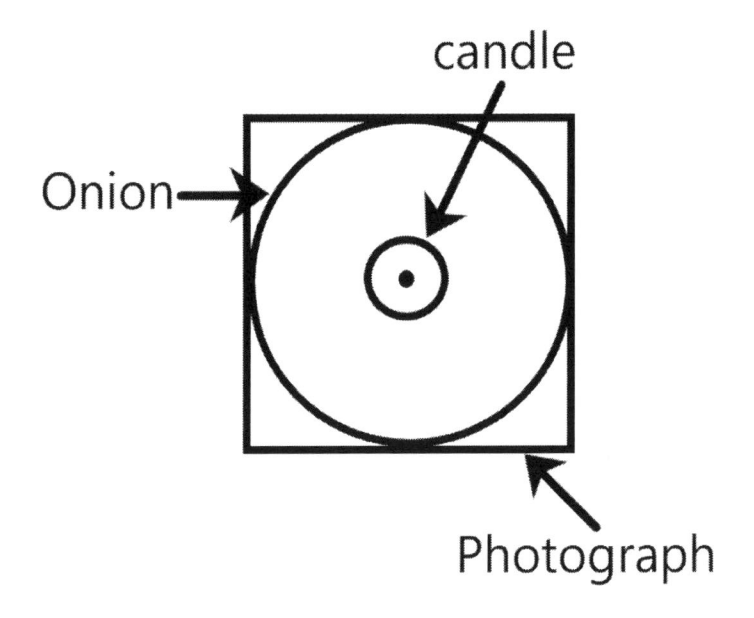

```
         candle
           ↓
Onion → ┌─────┐
        │  ◉  │
        │     │
        └─────┘
              ↑
         Photograph
```

- Light the candle and turn off the light.
- Say:

"I ask the Lords of War and Plague that weaken <u>NAME OF ENEMY</u> and put me always above and stronger than him".

- wait a few minutes in silence
- Sense the dark energy circling the ritual materials, and envision this dark energy weakening your enemy until he looks like an insect in comparison to you.
- Say it:

"I thank the Gods for the successful work"

- Leave the site
- Clean everything 24 hours later

ATTENTION: When disposing of materials, do not touch them, all work is full of destructive energy and therefore you should never touch the work after lighting the candle.

Put everything in a garbage bag without touching materials and dispose of them far away from your home.

Printed in Great Britain
by Amazon

1449f4a7-0592-4403-8ad9-99bd40c94524R01